Lou Reed
Between The Lines

Lou

Reed

Between The Lines

Michael Wrenn with Glen Marks

Plexus · London

All rights reserved including the right
of reproduction in whole or in part in any form
Copyright © 1993 by Plexus Publishing Limited
Published by Plexus Publishing Limited
26 Dafforne Road, London SW17 8TZ
First printing 1993

British Library Cataloguing-in-Publication Data
Wrenn, Michael
  Lou Reed: Between The Lines
  I.Title
  782.42166092

ISBN 0 85965 164 9

Designed by Phil Smee
Printed in Great Britain by J. W. Arrowsmith Ltd

10 9 8 7 6 5 4 3 2 1

Introduction

Acknowledgements

TRIP

ANDY WARHOL'S
PLASTIC INEVITABL
with the VELVET
UNDERGROUND & NIC
and the M.F.Q.

Introduction

'I DON'T UNDERSTAND A lot of the things people say to me about me. For instance, I don't understand why people call me the Godfather of Punk. They think I do, but I don't. All I ever wanted to do was to make records that adults could listen to without wincing, rather than all that rock, below-the-waist stuff. There's pop music, then there's what I do. I think of myself as a writer.' *Lou Reed*

'Hail Hail Rock'n'Roll! The Phantom of Rock!' proclaimed the advertisements for Lou Reed's first solo album, following his departure from the Velvet Underground some eighteen months earlier in the summer of 1970. It was a suitable announcement, and it still rings true today – getting on for thirty years since the group first emerged on the scene. Right up to the release of *Magic And Loss* in 1992, Lou Reed has continued to haunt dark shadows of the human condition, armed only with a thrusting electric guitar and a fistful of lyrics.

It seems amazing that although Lou Reed has been performing and recording for so many years, his reputation as a major rock musician and lyricist is still largely connected with the songs he wrote with the Velvet Underground. This commercially ignored, yet phenomenally influential group released only four studio albums in their original five year lifespan. From these Reed is best remembered for a handful of heavier numbers such as 'Heroin', 'White Light/White Heat', 'Waiting For The Man' and 'Sister Ray'. These songs have formed the basis for the belief that Lou Reed's music was purely and wholly concerned with sex, drugs and violence. Brilliant and stunning as they are, they remain a small part of Lou Reed's songbook. It is only now that critics, and the public alike, are responding to the softer and more positive side of Reed's music – a side that largely predominates.

Having turned 50 years old, Lou still stubbornly refuses to confine himself to current commercial trends and, although his rock and roll roots unmistakably remain, his work allies itself with a much more enduring art-form than the fickle sounds of youth-orientated pop culture. It is the duty of the artist to take risks, and one look at the ups and downs of Reed's career will show him to be a man never afraid to chance the difficult path – even when the easier one was being offered. There have been inevitable wrong turnings but, as he himself once observed, "My bullshit

_____derson

CLEAN LIVIN
AND
DIRTY LOOK

FLANKED BY his wife Sylvia
to his right and his
management on his left, Lou
Reed lords it over the press
gathering from a sofa dead
centre. Knowing he has just
20 minutes to consume in
the present company, he
sinks back and eases into a
lengthy, somewhat guarded
resume of his immediate
past, fleshed out by
digressions further back.

His reasoned, politician's
tone and measured
sentences proscribe
interruption from all but the
most ill-mannered lout, and
anyone who has the

before the competiti
level of questionin
resolutely on the
especially as th
corner to slink
hide behind or
impertinent qu
fired. And in kee
Reed's present c
sensibility there
available to lc
either his o

By all a
change
look p
clos
h

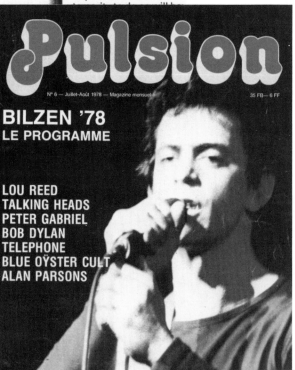

Pulsion

N° 6 — Juillet-Août 1978 — Magazine mensuel   35 FB - 6 FF

BILZEN '78
LE PROGRAMME

LOU REED
TALKING HEADS
PETER GABRIEL
BOB DYLAN
TELEPHONE
BLUE OŸSTER CULT
ALAN PARSONS

is other people's diamonds." Lou Reed was always the great survivor. Battered and bruised, maybe, but still firmly intact.

In Europe, Lou Reed has attracted a large and loyal audience over many years. It was these territories, particularly France and Italy, that helped keep him financially stable through the latter part of the 1970s, when his albums and concerts received scant attention in his homeland – but sold massively abroad. Things started changing in the mid-1980s. A series of consistently exciting and polished albums propelled him back into the international spotlight. Against all the odds, fighting and beating drug and alchohol addiction, Lou Reed remains honest and faithful to himself, his music and his public. After the knockout punches of *New York*, *Songs For Drella*, and *Magic And Loss* he is truly at the beginning of a new age.

What better way to tell the complete story of Lou Reed than from the words of the man himself. Often difficult and critical, his opinions are caustic, contentious and always compelling. It may be difficult sometimes to separate the fact from the fiction - just like his songs – as biographical details merge into fictional characters, and vice versa. But he walks it like he talks it. And what more can anyone ask?

Glen Marks

1. Coney Island Baby: 1942-1967

LEWIS ALLAN *Reed was born in Brooklyn, New York, on 2nd March 1942. At the age of eleven, when his father's legal accountancy business began to flourish, the family moved on to Freeport, Long Island, just down the road from Coney Island. The oldest of three children (Lou has a younger sister Elizabeth and, reportedly, a much younger brother – though nothing is known of him), Lou appears to have enjoyed a fairly normal early childhood. Keen on sports – especially basketball – he also developed an enthusiasm for the new rock-orientated radio stations that were continually emerging throughout his youth.*

'My parents were self-made millionaires. On paper they were very rich. I know what it's like to have money. They would love me to take over their companies. It's tax law – it all has to do with numbers. If United Steel is your client, you can save them millions.' *Lou Reed*

'Of course I'm Jewish, aren't all the best people?' *Lou Reed*

'I didn't want to grow up like my old man.' *Lou Reed*

Whatever the nature of Lou's grievance with his parents at this stage, they do seem to have encouraged the youngster's early enthusiasm for music, first lining up piano tuition, and then guitar lessons – albeit briefly. By the age of twelve, Lou was already composing imitation rockabilly and doo wop songs with a cousin.

'I was a tot – eight, ten, something like that. I just had a natural affinity for music. Playing the classical piano, I forgot all of it.' *Lou Reed*

'I started writing little classical pieces, but then I got bored with it.' *Lou Reed*

'I took classical music for fifteen fucking years, theory, composition, the whole thing. One of these days I'm gonna pull my degrees out and say, "Does that make me legitimate?"' *Lou Reed*

'My guitar teacher wanted to start normal lessons and I said, "No, no, no. Here's the record. Teach me how to play the chords for this record." And that was it. There are some advantages to not being schooled.' *Lou Reed*

'I got a guitar, a Gretsch Country Gentleman, and I paid somebody to teach me those first three chords. After that you're on your own, particularly at that time when you could play everything on the radio with those three chords.' *Lou Reed*

'I don't have that guitar anymore. I gave it away to a guy who used to trail after me all the time. He once said, "Why don't you give me your guitar? You never use it anymore." It was true, because I'd ruined it with some of the things I used to do. I built in two repeaters, right, and three tremelo units, plus all this other stuff, and then people magic markered it all up. By putting paint on the face they ruined the sound. And then one day [when playing with the Velvet Underground] I almost electrocuted myself with it, standing in a pool of beer out in The Hamptons. I literally levitated about three feet up. I said, "My God, let me outa here!" So this guy saw me with the guitar and said, "Can I have it?" And I said "Absolutely, just get it away from me. I advise you not to turn it on, you know?" ' *Lou Reed*

Lou played in a succession of bands while still at school, and looked to pick up tips about how to progress as a musician from Allen Fredericks, a DJ who presented 'The Night Train' show on the local radio station. The first group Lou actually recorded with was the Shades, later renamed the Jades, to avoid confusion with another New York group of the period. In 1957, when Lou was still only fifteen, they recorded a single, 'So Blue'/ 'Leave Her For Me', on the Time label and, although it was picked up by the more prominent Dot Records, the release failed to make an impression and the band was dropped.

'The Jades wasn't a band, it was just one guitar and two other guys singing. I was in the background. I wrote the stuff, I didn't sing it. We would play shopping malls and

A COLLECTOR'S ITEM: THE JADES' ONLY SINGLE, 'SO BLUE/LEAVE HER FOR ME'.

some really bad violent places. I was always, like, tremendously under age, which was pretty cool. [When recording] our lead singer had to stand on a box so he could reach the microphone, 'cause they had a very big black guy singing the harmony

parts with the rest of us. I'll always remember he was huge, and he had a giant mound of snot hanging out of his nose and we were too afraid to tell him.' *Lou Reed*

But that wasn't the only thing Lou was scared of. Ever since the time he entered his teens, the youngster had realised his sexuality wasn't in tune with the norm, and he quickly learned to cover up his attraction to male contemporaries.

'I resent it. It was a very big drag. From age twelve on I could have been having a ball and not even thought about this shit. What a waste of time. If the forbidden thing is love, then you spend most of your time playing with hate. Who needs that? I feel I was gypped.' *Lou Reed*

When Lou's parents became aware of their son's alternative sexuality, they arranged for him to be given electric-shock therapy as a way of irradicating his socially unacceptable homosexual tendencies. He was seventeen years old. Lou's father had apparently been so appalled by Lou's sexual preferences, he was prepared to go to all lengths to straighten him out. The result was a family rift which would reportedly last for the next 20 years.

'They put the thing down your throat so you don't swallow your tongue, and they put electrodes on your head. That's what was recommended in Rockland County then to discourage homosexual feelings. The effect is that you lose your memory and become a vegetable. I wrote "Kill Your Sons" on *Sally Can't Dance* about that. You can't read a book because you get to page seventeen and have to go right back to page one again.' *Lou Reed*

Music became an escape for the persecuted youngster throughout his teens, and Lou digested everything that was thrown at him.

'I was influenced by everybody, by all the rock'n'roll I ever heard – the street groups, old fifties rock. I always liked all those really corny lyrics.' *Lou Reed*

By the autumn of 1961, the nineteen-year-old Reed eventually managed to escape from his suburban existence – to Syracuse University, where he took a degree in Literature and Philosophy. It was here that he came into contact with Delmore Schwartz, the influential Jewish poet and short-story writer, whose work explored the relationship between private self and the outside world. His book of stories and poems, In Dreams Begin Responsibilities *(1937), is one of modern America's most highly-acclaimed works. Schwartz was now on a downward, alcoholic spiral of lecturing and reminiscing on former glories. Still a charismatic figure in middle age – and still highly thought of by contemporaries Saul Bellow and Robert Lowell, who were both instrumental in his appointment at Syracuse – Schwartz had a profound influence on the young and impressionable Reed.*

'Delmore Schwartz was the unhappiest man who I ever met in my life, and the smartest – till I met Andy Warhol. He didn't use curse words until he was thirty. His mother wouldn't allow him. His worst fears were realised when he died [in 1966] and they put him in a plot next to her. Once, drunk in a Syracuse bar, he said, "If you sell out, Lou, I'm gonna get ya." I hadn't thought about doing anything, let alone selling out. Two years later he was gone. I'm just delighted I got to know him. It would have been tragic not to have met him. But things have occurred where Delmore's words float right across. Very few people do it to you. He was one.' *Lou Reed*

'Delmore's *In Dreams Begin Responsibilities* really was amazing to me. To think you could do that with the simplest words available in such a short span of pages and create something so incredibly powerful. You could write something like that and not have the greatest vocabulary in the world.' *Lou Reed*

'I just thought that Delmore was the greatest. We drank together starting at eight in the morning. He was an awesome person. He'd order five drinks at once. He was incredibly smart. He could recite the encyclopedia to you. He was also one of the funniest people I ever met in my life.' *Lou Reed*

Making the most of being away from home, Lou enjoyed his first gay love affair during his inaugural year at college.

'It was just the most amazing experience. It was never consummated. I felt very bad about it because I had a girlfriend and I was always going out on the side – and subterfuge is not my hard-on. I couldn't figure out what was wrong. I wanted to fix it up and make it OK. I figured that if I sat around and thought about it I could straighten it out.' *Lou Reed*

Lou began writing poetry at college, and tried hard to get his work published.

'*The New Yorker* rejected me. That's when I wanted to be a New Yorker poet. I used to get Writer's Market which told you all the books that take poetry, like the *Kenyon Review, Hudson Review, Paris Review*, but later it dawned on me, who wants to be published in these magazines anyway?' *Lou Reed*

'Lou's the only guy I've ever known who could improvise words that actually made sense when analysed afterwards.' *John Cale*

'I always wanted to be a writer and I went to college to prepare myself for it. See, that's where I'm coming from. If you have my interests and my kind of academic background, then what I'm doing is not really an unlikely thing to do.' *Lou Reed*

'I didn't care for the academic life at all. That's not to put it down – some people love it. But I didn't.' *Lou Reed*

Campus life however, was another matter altogether, and Lou grabbed every opportunity that came his way – he even hosted his own jazz show on college radio. He didn't only enjoy the chance of broadening his horizons artistically, but also met people who could help him put his new ideas into practice. At Syracuse he met Sterling Morrison through a mutual friend, Jim Tucker. Sterling Morrison had already tried two other colleges before visiting Syracuse with a view to signing up as a student there. In fact he never did, remaining as a literature student at City College of New York. He immediately hit it off with Lou. The pair quickly became sidekicks in a whole string of student bands. It was at this time too, that Lou really started to experiment with drugs.

'I was introduced to drugs by a mashed-in-faced Negro whose features were in two sections, like a split-level house, named Jaw. Jaw gave me hepatitis immediately, which is pathetic and laughable at once, considering I wrote a famous amplified version of the experience as a song. Anyway, his bad blood put an end to my abortive excursions . . .' *Lou Reed*

'The colleges have to be destroyed. They're dangerous. Doctors trying to cure the freaks while they gulp pills. Rushing with the music. It's the music that kept us all intact . . . kept us from going crazy. You [all] should have two radios in case one gets broken.' *Lou Reed*

'Lou and I had some of the shittiest bands that ever were. They were shitty because they were playing authentic rock'n'roll. Lou and I came from the identical environment of Long Island rock'n'roll bars, where you can drink anything at eighteen, and everybody had phony proof of their age at sixteen.' *Sterling Morrison*

After graduating in the summer of 1964, Lou

decided to remain a Syracuse student for a while, putting down for a postgraduate course in journalism. Later he switched to drama.

'I dropped out of journalism school after a week. I had just learned the triangular paragraph, and then I gave an opinion. The critique that came back said, "You interjected your opinion, that's not what you're supposed to be doing." And I quit.' *Lou Reed*

'I went to journalists' school for a short while . . . It was like being on a mental ski-slope. Then I went to drama school. I played the part of a dead body.' *Lou Reed*

'As an actor I couldn't cut it – I couldn't cut the mustard as they say. But I was good as a director.' *Lou Reed*

While undertaking these postgraduate courses, Lou continued to play in a succession of local bands.

'I made more money being in bar bands up in Syracuse, than I ever made in the Velvet Underground. We were pretty bad, and we had to change our name a lot. We played fraternities. People would vomit on your amp.' *Lou Reed*

By this time the Vietnam draft was in full swing, yet miraculously Lou managed to fail his interview for the unenviable posting. If it wasn't due to his hepatitis, it's possible he played the homosexual card, but whatever the reason for his unacceptability, Lou wasn't drafted.

'I was pronounced mentally unfit by the draft board, and have a classification that means I'll only be called up if we go to war with China. I did it well, I was only in the interview for about ten minutes.' *Lou Reed*

'I was drafted and I got out of it, as crazy. But that's not something to be proud of. I managed to get out of it, as almost everybody I knew did. But I think about it. There's a moral dilemma that goes along with that.' *Lou Reed*

Instead of joining up, Lou went to work at Pickwick Records' New York office in October 1964, where he was paid to compose conveyor belt pastiches of all the major hits of the period.

'I went to work as a songwriter for Pickwick. We just churned out songs, that's all. Never a hit song – what we were doing was churning out these rip-off albums. In other words the album would say it featured four groups, it would just be various permutations of us, and they would sell them at supermarkets for 99 cents or a dollar. While I was doing that I was doing my own stuff and trying to get by, but the material I was doing, people wouldn't go near me with it at the time. I mean we wrote "Johnny Can't Surf No More" and "Let The Wedding Bells Ring" and "Hot Rod Song".' *Lou Reed*

Working at this end of the business, Reed certainly had good cause to grow quickly cynical about the music industry. But that didn't mean he was unable to appreciate the genuine talents of those who'd cracked it without having to go through the same soul-destroying process.

'The Beatles were innocent of the world and its wicked ways, while I no longer possessed this pristine view. I, after all, had had jaundice.' *Lou Reed*

'The Beatles just make the songs up, bing, bing, bing. They have to be the most incredible songwriters ever – just amazingly talented. I don't think people realise how sad it is that the Beatles broke up.' *Lou Reed*

While at Pickwick during the early weeks of 1965, Lou found himself in an embarrassing situation when one of his company's fictitious bands (the Primitives) was invited to play on the popular TV show 'American Bandstand'. Turning negative into positive however, Lou and

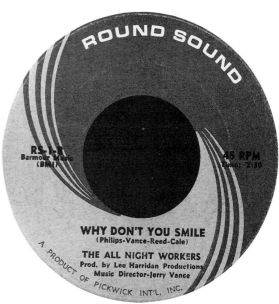

A PICKWICK PRODUCT FROM REED, CALE AND FRIENDS. THE BACKING SOUNDS LIKE 'VENUS IN FURS' BUT FRONTED BY A BLACK SOUL SINGER.

his Pickwick colleague Terry Phillips decided to get a band together, joining forces with a couple of people Terry had met at a party. These were Tony Conrad and John Cale. Tony Conrad was a young musician who shared an apartment and an interest in experimental music with John Cale, the classically trained son of a Welsh miner who had arrived in New York via a scholarship to Tanglewood, one of America's most renowned music colleges. Cale's interest in the avant-garde, particularly his work with the renowned visionary LaMonte Young, whose rarely recorded work has inspired composers like Philip Glass and Steve Reich, had a tremendous impact on the 22-year-old Reed. For his part, Cale was quite struck by Lou's lyrics, particularly in a song he'd just written – 'Heroin'.

'I met Lou at a party. I had long hair and Lou said I looked commercial. He was trying to get a band together. I didn't want to hear his songs – they seemed sorry for themselves. Eventually he showed me the lyrics, which had some really perceptive things in them.' *John Cale*

'I decided to make up a dance, so I said,

"You put your head on the floor and have somebody step on it." It was years ahead of its time.' *Lou Reed on his promotional ideas with The Primitives*

Following a brief spell as the Primitives, Reed and Cale decided to maintain the connection, being re-joined by Sterling Morrison in a new line-up augmented by percussionist Angus Maclise. Throughout the first half of 1965 they tried out a variety of names such as the Warlocks and the Falling Spikes. They were then invited to provide a soundtrack for a short film, Venus In Furs, *directed by an underground film-maker,*

COLLEGE BOY: A CLEAN-CUT LOU REED PLAYS AT SYRACUSE UNIVERSITY IN 1963.

Piero Heliczer, who had been at school with Maclise at Forest Hills High School in the mid-fifties. Lou Reed's own 'Venus In Furs' – a flirtation with sexual masochism – provided the principal musical backdrop.

'I saw the book *Venus In Furs* [by Leopold von Sacher-Masoch] and just thought it would be a great idea for a song. Now everybody thinks I invented masochism.' *Lou Reed talking about the inspiration for 'Venus in Furs', from the* Velvet Underground And Nico *album*

Things were beginning to look quite good for the band by the end of 1965, until the eccentric

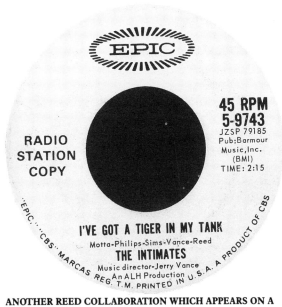

EPIC

RADIO
STATION
COPY

45 RPM
5-9743
JZSP 79185
Pub:Barmour
Music,Inc.
(BMI)
TIME: 2:15

I'VE GOT A TIGER IN MY TANK
Motta-Philips-Sims-Vance-Reed
THE INTIMATES
Music director-Jerry Vance
An ALH Production
T.M. PRINTED IN U.S.A. A PRODUCT OF CBS

EPIC··CBS. MARCAS REG.

ANOTHER REED COLLABORATION WHICH APPEARS ON A PICKWICK LP CREDITED TO THE BEECHNUTS BUT WITH DIFFERENT WORDS. PICKWICK WAS AN EARLY EXPONENT OF RECYCLING – IF IT DIDN'T WORK ONE WAY, RECYCLE THE MUSIC WITH A NEW SET OF LYRICS.

Maclise suddenly quit and went to India. He had anyway expressed reservations about 'gigging' which involved playing to a set time and programme. But they needed a drummer in a hurry. Jim Tucker's sister Maureen was immediately available – so she was in. Following an invitation from music journalist and would-be entrepreneur Al Aronowitz, the Velvet Underground played their first ever show on 12th December 1965 at Summit High School, New Jersey – as support act for the Aronowitz-managed, and appallingly named, Myddle Class.

'We needed an amplifier and she had one, plus she's an out of sight drummer. She worked as a computer key-puncher and, when she'd come home at five, she'd put on Bo Diddley records and play every night from five to 12. So we figured she'd be the perfect drummer, and she was.' *Lou Reed*

'I can remember Lou coming to the house once when I was in the 12th grade. Then Sterling went up to Syracuse to look around, he and Lou started playing, and that was kind of the beginning. The show came up at

Summit High School and Angus was out, so they said, "Let's get Tucker's sister, she likes to play drums."' *Mo Tucker*

'Maureen Tucker is so beautiful. She has to be one of the most fantastic people I've ever met in my life. She's so impossibly great.' *Lou Reed*

It was at this time also that Tony Conrad showed the band another book – a trashy sex exposé by Michael Leigh entitled The Velvet Underground. *Everyone agreed that this would be a perfect name for the band, hinting at the band's links with the progressive avant garde.*

Al Aronowitz came to a loose arrangement with the Velvet Underground regarding their representation, and gave them a good deal of encouragement, as well as advice as to how they might present their work to a captive audience. They generally played a mixture of Reed's own compositions and Chuck Berry covers, and this was basically the same set that they presented at the Cafe Bizarre in Greenwich Village later the same

month where Aronowitz had set them up in a residency. It was at the Cafe Bizarre that Andy Warhol first saw them. They were sacked two days later.

'When we first put the Velvets together, we formed a group around the guitar, bass, drums and my electric viola. We wanted the Velvet Underground to be a group with a dynamic symphonic flair. The idea was that Lou's lyrical and melodic ability could be combined with some of my musical ideas to create performances where we wouldn't just repeat ourselves . . . In the beginning, when Al Aronowitz was managing us and we were playing at the Bizarre, we practised a lot and were pretty tight.' *John Cale*

'They said – "One more song like that and you're fired." So we played one more song like that and, sure enough, they fired us.' *Lou Reed, on the completion of their residency at Cafe Bizarre, following one too many renditions of 'Black Angel's Death Song'.*

'I was very taken aback when people were surprised when the Velvet Underground consciously set out to put themes common to movies, plays and novels into a pop song format . . . I have songs about killing people, but Dostoevsky killed people too. In reality I might not do what a character in my songs would do if only because I'd be jailed. I've always thought it would be kinda fun to introduce people to characters they maybe hadn't met before, or hadn't wanted to meet . . . It's simply professional detachment. You could say I'm a voyeur, but I'm not. I'm just talking about what goes on around me. I've always been listening. The way things happen is the way they are. They're not necessarily about me though. That's where everybody gets confused.' *Lou Reed*

'When Lou and I started the group, there was a basic understanding . . . it seemed more important to be different than immediately successful, to have a personality of

our own, to have arrangements like "Venus In Furs", and to give concerts that were never the same.' *John Cale*

'I went through this stage where I was writing down all the weird things that people were saying.' *Lou Reed*

Reed wasn't just writing them down, but inventing them too, as can be seen from this attempt to describe the inevitable rise of the Velvet Underground:

'Of course it had to happen, it was the natural end to Beethoven's Ninth. Everybody was getting sicker and looking like wolverine . . . Dirty buildings with lawns for people to lie on blankets . . . But meanwhile everything was dead, movies were dead. Writing was dead, movies were dead. Everyone sat like an unpeeled orange. But the music was so beautiful . . .' *Lou Reed*

'One of my strong points is that I'm good at dialogue. I can make it sound like something someone said. A lot of my stuff sounds like the way people speak, when in fact it's not.

It's sort of a polished version of the way people speak.' *Lou Reed*

Andy Warhol, the celebrated pop artist, was looking for a band to reflect the mood of his experimental work in film and performance art, and no-one could come closer than the Velvet Underground. Not surprisingly then, Warhol offered the band a management contract within days of their first meeting. The Velvets decided it was an offer they shouldn't refuse. The deal was a simple one; Andy would put up the money to buy any equipment the group required, as well as providing regular rehearsal space. In return the band would have to make themselves available to him whenever they were required. By the end of December 1965 the deal was signed.

'Lou Reed was playing at the Cafe Bizarre, and Barbara Rubin, a friend of Jonas Mekas, said she knew this group. Claes Oldenburg and Lucas Samaras and Jasper Johns and I were starting a rock'n'roll group with people like LaMonte Young, and the artist who digs holes in the desert now, Walter DeMaria. We met ten times, and there were fights between Lucas and Patti over the music or something . . . I was singing badly. Then Barbara Rubin said something about this group, and mixed-media was getting to be the big thing at the Cinematheque, so . . .' *Andy Warhol*

'We worked with lights and stuff behind us before we met Andy. We did it in the old Cinematheque on Lafayette Street. It wasn't his original conception. It was a lot of people's conception. It was a natural step to meet Andy and say, "Oh, you've got a week at the new Cinematheque" so obviously since we combined music with movies and everything it was just such an easy step to say, "We'll play along with your movies." Then we said, "You've got all these things. Why don't we show lights?" It doesn't matter whose idea it was. It was just so obvious. It wasn't Andy putting it all together. It was everybody. It was just Andy had the week at the Cinematheque. That's what Andy had to do, and then everybody put it together. The thing was that the basic idea was so obvious that you would have to be a fool not to think of it.' *Lou Reed*

'Andy told me that what we were doing with music was the same thing he was doing with painting and movies and writing, ie, not kidding around. To my mind nobody in music was doing anything that even approximated the real thing, with the exception of us. We were doing a specific thing that was very, very real. It wasn't slick or a lie in any conceivable way, which was the only way we could work with him. Because the first thing I liked about Andy was that he was very real.' *Lou Reed*

'All the songs for the first Velvet Underground album were written before I ever met [Warhol]. It's just that they happened to match his thing perfectly.' *Lou Reed*

Lou was impressed by Andy, and spent as much time as possible at the artist's New York studio, known as the Factory. During the next eighteen months Lou soaked up the whole scene, learning not just from Warhol, but also from the extraordinary collection of people in the artist's entourage. The influence was not purely an intellectual one however, and Lou very quickly began to dress in the work-place uniform of black leather and

THE VELVET UNDERGROUND – CAPTURED BY GERARD MALANGA – ALMOST REMEMBERING TO SMILE. L. TO R.: MAUREEN TUCKER, STERLING MORRISON, LOU REED AND JOHN CALE.

shades. *Long term, the events and characters would ultimately inspire Reed's 'Walk On The Wild Side'.*

'If you want to know all about Andy Warhol, just look at the surface, of my paintings and films and me, and there I am. There's nothing behind it.' *Andy Warhol*

'If you want to know what I am, look at the surface. Because I'm inside.' *Lou Reed*

'Lou Reed, who always had this incredible, menacing scowl on his face, wouldn't say more than one or two syllables, because that was how Andy Warhol was.' *Jackson Brown*

Warhol decided there was something missing from the band and chose to fill the gap with Nico, a former model and one-time actress. Born in Hungary (possibly as early as 1940) to Spanish and Yugoslav parents, Nico's educational background in France and Italy was impressive. She learned to speak seven languages, and would have moved into a long-term movie career had her parents not prevented her from signing a contract with the director Federico Fellini. She was ultimately introduced to Warhol by Bob Dylan, who is reported to have fallen under her spell.

Lou was not happy about the introduction of Nico, and the fact that she gave John Cale more attention than Lou Reed didn't help. Nico's involvement would spell trouble from day one.

'Andy decided to throw Nico into the act because the Velvets themselves were not very charismatic on stage, and Andy wanted a spotlight on someone. So Andy threw her in on the act against the wishes of the Velvets, actually.' *Gerard Malanga, Factory hand, poet and actor.*

Poor Richard's
— PRESENTS —
ANDY WARHOL AND HIS
EXPLODING PLASTIC
INEVITABLE (SHOW)

★ ★ ★ ★ ★ ★ FEATURING ★ ★ ★ ★ ★ ★ ★

THE NEW SOUND OF THE
VELVET UNDERGROUND

★ ★ ★ ★ ★ ★ WITH ★ ★ ★ ★ ★ ★

★ NICO – Pop Girl of '66

★ ★

JUNE 21 thru JUNE 26

POOR RICHARD'S
1363 NO. SEDGWICK ★
(OLD TOWN)
Tele. 337-1497 After 3 P.M.

— SHOWS —
10:00 P.M.
12:00 P.M. & 2 A.M.

RESERVATIONS
REQUIRED

'Nico is the kind of person that you meet, and you're not quite the same afterwards . . . She has an amazing mind. She isn't the type of person who stays very long in any one country. Nico's fantastic. She always understood immediately what I was after with a song.' *Lou Reed*

'Lou likes to manipulate women, you know, like program them. He wanted to do that with me . . . He told me so. Like computerise me.' *Nico*

'Nico is half goddess, half icicle. If you say bad things about her singing, she doesn't talk to you. If you say nice things, she doesn't talk to you either . . .' *Richard Goldstein*

Part of the problem with Nico, as far as Lou was concerned, was her obsession with Bob Dylan.

The latter had composed a song especially for Nico, entitled 'I'll Keep It With Mine', a number she was keen to sing with the Velvet Underground. In New York during this period there was intense rivalry between the Dylan and Warhol camps.

'We most certainly did not want to be compared with Bob Dylan, or associated with him. We did not want to be near Bob Dylan, either physically, or through his songs. When Nico kept insisting that we work up "I'll Keep It With Mine", for a long time we simply refused. Then we took a long time to learn it – as long as we could take. After that, even though we knew the song, we insisted that we were unable to play it. When we finally did have a go at it on stage, it was performed poorly. We never got any better at it either, for some reason.' *Sterling Morrison*

'Dylan gets on my nerves. If you were at a party with him, I think you'd tell him to shut up.' *Lou Reed*

'Dylan was *never* around for me. But he did have a nice flair for words that didn't mean anything. They were just marijuana throwaways.' *Lou Reed*

Certainly Dylan and Reed were setting different goals for themselves during this period . . .

'The Velvet Underground was a whole other dimension. New York, New York, sweetheart, strung-out, vicious and twitching in spangled pants and see-through shirts coming into your living room to destroy your middle-class sense of propriety and well-being.' *Robert Greenfield*

By the time Nico joined forces with the Velvet Underground (and well before the release of their debut album), Lou Reed had already gained considerable notoriety for the inspired nature of his songwriting.

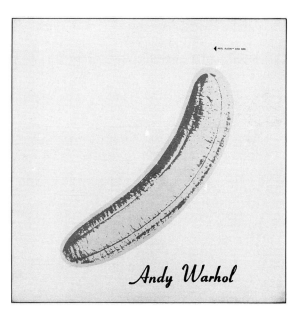

THE RARE ORIGINAL WARHOL SLEEVE FOR *THE VELVET UNDERGROUND AND NICO* WITH PEELABLE BANANA SKIN (THE BANANA UNDERNEATH IS PINK).

'All the bastards that you were supposed to feel sorry for, and fight wars for, were screaming, "Look at the freaks in Central Park with transistors up their heads." ' *Lou Reed, in defence of the Velvet Underground's 'alternative' image*

And again, in early defence of the band's drug-tinged lyrics . . .

'If someone's dumb enough to take heroin just because they heard a song, it's not my responsibility.' *Lou Reed*

'Rock fans have taken heroin thinking Lou took heroin, forgetting that the character in the song "Heroin" wasn't necessarily Lou Reed.' *Sterling Morrison*

'There's always this thing about saying that the artist is it, that he's what he is singing. I sang so many different characters that I thought people would understand that I couldn't be all of them. I had to be the writer behind them, and I could write or sing a song I disagreed with totally, but that I understood people who were that way, or maybe one minute part of me might be that way, and I could blow it up, you know what I mean?' *Lou Reed*

'I did go down Lexington – I did all the stuff then.' *Lou Reed, in reference to the Velvets' 'Waiting For The Man'.*

The Velvet Underground and Nico performed live for the first time at New York's Delmonico Hotel on 8 January 1966. Meanwhile Andy Warhol was already making plans for the band to spearhead his mixed-media event, Uptight *(launched in February 1966), a forerunner to the notorious theatrical extravaganza –* The Exploding Plastic Inevitable *(the new title being invented by Factory assistant Paul Morrissey the following month), said by many critics to represent performance art in its most perverse form. A glance at an edition of the* Fire Island News *during this period gives a clearer insight into how the performances were viewed . . .*

'The rock and roll music gets louder, the dancers get more frantic, and the lights start going on and off like crazy. And there are spotlights blinking in our eyes, and car horns beeping, and Gerard Malanga and the dancers are shaking like mad, and you don't think the noise can get any louder, and then it does, until there is one big rhythmic tidal

YOU GET THE BENDS!

What happens when the daddy of Pop Art goes Pop Music? The most underground album of all! It's Andy Warhol's hip new trip to the current subterranean scene.

Sorry, no home movies. But the album does feature Andy's Velvet Underground (they play funny instruments). Plus his this year's Pop Girl, Nico (she sings, groovy). Plus an actual Warhol banana on the front cover (don't smoke it...peel it)!

The Velvet Underground, produced by Andy Warhol, is now available at record stores across the country. Just bring your own plain brown wrapper.

Verve Records is a division of Metro-Goldwyn-Mayer Inc.

wave of sound, pressing down around you, just impure enough so you can still get the best; the audience, the dancers, the music and the movies, all of it fused together into one magnificent moment of hysteria.' *George English*

'The term "Exploding Plastic Inevitable" came from sitting around with Gerard [Malanga] and Barbara Rubin, thinking of a name. I picked up a record with Barbara on the back, massaging Bob Dylan's head (*Bringing It All Back Home*). There were some amphetamine Bob Dylan gibberish liner notes. I looked without reading and saw these words appear. Something was "exploding", something was "plastic", something was "inevitable". I said, "Why not call it 'Exploding Plastic Inevitable – The Velvet Underground And Nico"?' *Paul Morrissey, film-maker and Warhol side-kick*

'People would tell us it was violent, it was grotesque, it was perverted. We said, "What are you talking about. It's fun. Look at

all these people having fun" . . . A lot of those people are dead now, or they're in institutions. It was quite a combination of people . . .' *Lou Reed talking about the Exploding Plastic Inevitable tour*

'If they can take it for ten minutes, then play it for fifteen. That's our policy. Always leave them wanting less.' *Andy Warhol*

'In our show, the guy who was doing the lights, Danny Williams – he committed suicide eventually – he would sit up for hours at the Factory, with seven strobe lights, and use himself as a test subject. That's why John and I used to wear sunglasses when we played. We didn't want to see it.' *Lou Reed*

'We all knew something revolutionary was happening. We just felt it. Things couldn't look this strange and new without some barrier being broken. "It's like the Red Seeea," Nico said, standing next to me one

night on the Dom Balcony that looked out over all the action, "paaaaarting".' *Andy Warhol*

'The show was like eating a banana nut Brillopad.' *David Crosby*

'We have these problems with a very enthusiastic audience that yells and screams and throws fits and tantrums and rolls on the floor . . . and they walked out into the street, and they still had these vibrations in their ears, especially the last song, called "Nothing Song", which was just noise and feedback and screeches and groans . . .' *Lou Reed*

'If this is what America's waiting for, we are all going to die of boredom, because this is a celebration of the silliness of cafe society . . . The Velvet Underground was really pretty lame . . . Camp plus con equals nothing.' *Ralph J. Gleason of the* San Francisco Chronicle, *after seeing the Velvet Underground perform in 1966.*

In Los Angeles the EPI show was banned, but the group got paid anyway. With the takings, the Velvet Underground went into the studio to record 'Heroin', 'All Tomorrow's Parties', 'Waiting For

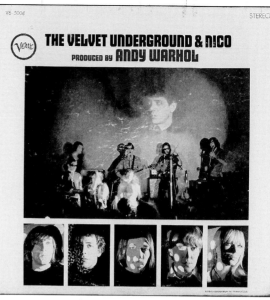

THE BACK OF THE FIRST VELVET UNDERGROUND ALBUM SLEEVE – WHICH WAS USED AS THE FRONT IN THE UK – SHOWS THE GROUP LIVE AND IN FULL FLIGHT, COMPLETE WITH LIGHT SHOW. ORIGINAL USA COPIES ALSO HAVE AN INVERTED ANGEL/DANCER IN THE BACKGROUND.

The Man' and 'Venus in Furs'. On the strength of these sessions the Velvet Underground attracted a deal with MGM's Verve label – who had also signed Frank Zappa's Mothers of Invention. Much to Reed's fury, the company prioritised the Mothers' Freak Out album and delayed on the

MAUREEN TUCKER

STERLING MORRISON

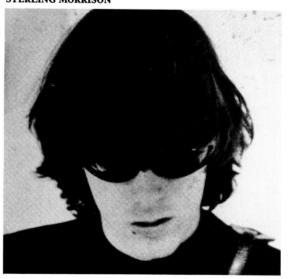

26

Velvet Underground record which, although completed by the summer of 1966, wasn't released until the spring of the following year. (Reed never seems to have forgiven Zappa for that one.) Simply titled The Velvet Underground And Nico, *the album gained immediate recognition, not so much for the music, but for Andy Warhol's phallic banana design on the cover. Warhol was also credited as the producer on the album, but this appears to be principally a marketing ploy,*

LOU REED

since Tom Wilson (credited as the 'engineer') is widely understood to have done most of the work.

'The West Coast bands were into soft drugs. We were into hard drugs.' *Lou Reed*

'We had vast objections to the whole San Francisco scene. It's just tedious, a lie and untalented. They can't play and they certainly can't write. I keep telling everybody and nobody cares. We used to be quiet, but I don't even care any more about not

THE VELVET UNDERGROUND AND NICO

NICO AND JOHN CALE

wanting to say negative things, 'cause things have gone so far that somebody should really say something. You know, people like Jefferson Airplane, Grateful Dead, all those people are just the most untalented bores that ever came up. Just look at them physically, I mean, can you take Grace Slick seriously? It's a joke, it's a joke, the kids are being hyped.' *Lou Reed*

'You know, you always amplify things you're reflecting. I was thinking things seemed so negative, so things we were putting down were rough, but it was what it was really all about.' *Lou Reed, on the first Velvets album.*

'We were trying to do a Phil Spector thing with as few instruments as possible. On some tracks it worked. "Venus In Furs" is the best, and "All Tomorrow's Parties" and "Sunday Morning". The band never again

TIM BUCKLEY
VELVET UNDERGROUND
ALL MEN JOY
JERRY ABRAMS HEADLIGHTS
AVALON BALLROOM
Sutter & Van Ness ❧ JULY 19, 20, 21

had as good a producer as Tom Wilson. He did those songs, plus "Heroin" and "Waiting For My Man". [Sic.] They were done in LA at Cameo-Parkway. Andy Warhol didn't do anything. The rest were done by a businessman who came up with $1500 for us to go into a broken down studio and record the thing. I wasn't writing songs until Lou and I did "Little Sister" for Nico's *Chelsea Girls* LP. Whenever Lou and I worked together, I'd play piano and he would flip whatever version he had around it. I didn't contribute lyrics to any of his songs; he contributed to some of mine. We collaborated slightly on "Sunday Morning", "Black Angel's Death Song" and, later, "Lady Godiva's Operation". Most of it would be written, but a small part would be unresolved – and Lou would resolve it.' *John Cale*

'The prosaic truth about "Venus In Furs" is that I'd read a book with this title by Leopold Sacher-Masoch and I thought it would make a great song title, so I had to write a song to go with it. But it's not necessarily what I'm into.' *Lou Reed*

'Andy made a point of trying to make sure that on our first album the language remained intact. I think Andy was interested in shocking, in giving people a jolt and not to let them talk us into making compromises. He said, "Oh you've got to make sure you leave the dirty words in." He was adamant about that. He didn't want it to be cleaned up and, because he was there, it wasn't. And, as a consequence of that, we always knew what it was like to have your way . . .' *Lou Reed*

'I'm not advocating anything. It all happened quite simply at the start. It's just that we had "Heroin", "Waiting For My Man", [sic.] and "Venus In Furs", all on the first album, and that just about set the tone. It's like we also had "Sunday Morning", which was so pretty, and "I'll Be Your Mirror", but

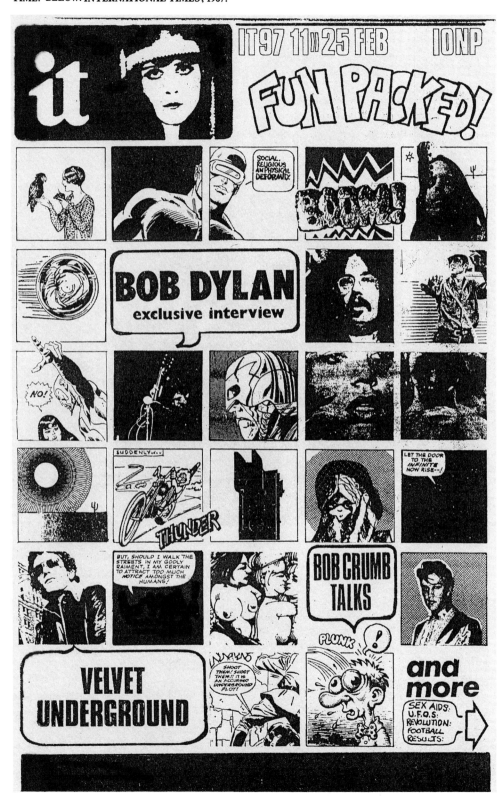

THE SINGLE 'SUNDAY MORNING',
TAKEN FROM THE FIRST VELVETS LP.
AN EARLY ATTEMPT AT 'MARKETING'
WHICH FALTERED AS VERVE ONLY ISSUED A FEW COPIES
OF THE SINGLE.

everyone psyched into the other stuff.' *Lou Reed*

'Andy mentioned that some of the records we're doing end up sounding so professional. No-one wants it to sound professional. It's so much nicer to play into one very cheap mike. That's the way it sounds when you hear it live, and that's the way it should sound on the record.' *Lou Reed*

'When the record came out I was very excited. I ran out to the store and bought one. They gave me a copy, but I wanted to buy one. Finding it in stores was nice, but

that didn't last long because MGM fucked up. They didn't really distribute it at all. But I was very excited, and Sterling was too, as I recall, and I'm sure John and Lou were thrilled.' *Mo Tucker*

'As soon as the record came out, the Velvets didn't want to work any more. They thought they became very famous when their album was finally released. I think they just wanted to separate from Andy, although we went on tour with them all over the country! I forget

who booked that tour but, God Almighty, I could never forget that gruelling ordeal on the buses. We were going on buses!'
Paul Morrissey

A young club owner named Steve Sesnick began to be interested in the Velvet Underground, believing they needed more formalised representation than Warhol could provide. Based in Boston, Sesnick had become a fan of the band after seeing them play there at regular intervals, and in May 1967 he invited the group to play at his ballroom, the Boston Tea Party. With Warhol away at the Cannes Film Festival, and Nico committed to solo engagements elsewhere (she'd already declared an intention to pursue a solo career), the booking cleared the way for the band to develop its identity away from Warhol's 'Exploding Plastic Inevitable'. And although Nico actually turned up towards the end of the Velvets set, she was refused admission to the stage by the other band members, claiming she had no real role in the proceedings. The writing, as they say, was clearly on the wall.

'I have a habit of leaving places at the wrong time, just when something big might have happened for me.' *Nico*

Initially Sesnick is said to have tried to get the Velvet Underground a deal (as a four-piece) with the Beatles' manager Brian Epstein but, when this failed, Sesnick decided to make a move himself (with Reed's approval) and the Velvet Underground accepted his offer in the early summer of 1967. Warhol was visibly hurt.

'Andy [Warhol] called me a rat. It was the worst thing he could think of.' *Lou Reed*

'When [Andy and I] worked together, we were very close. It was just people working to get onto something. The thing is that Andy works very hard. One of the things you can learn from being at the Factory is, if you want to do whatever you do, then you should work very very hard. If you don't work very hard all the time, then nothing

will happen. And Andy works as hard as anybody I know. He used to say things to me that were involved around our working. Whenever he'd ask me how many songs were written that day, whatever the number was, Andy would say, "You should do more." . . . Working with him was really fantastic. We worked until the [Exploding Plastic Inevitable] show couldn't exist anymore, because it was just so expensive.'
Lou Reed

'We all just felt that [Sesnick] was more our style. There were a couple of other guys lurking – and they wanted to manage us – but they were just too businessy, and I think we thought that we wouldn't relate to them too well . . . And Sesnick was very enthusiastic.' *Mo Tucker*

'I remember Brian Epstein best for a story that may or may not have been true. In his mansion he kept Spanish servants, none of who could speak English. Let that be a lesson to us all in discretion.' *Lou Reed*

A VELVET UNDERGROUND BOOTLEG ALBUM FEATURING THE JACKET DESIGN OF THE ORIGINAL PAPERBACK BOOK, *THE VELVET UNDERGROUND* BY MICHAEL LEE, FROM WHICH THE GROUP TOOK THEIR NAME.

THE VELVET UNDERGROUND AND NICO

Once details were finalised, mainly through Lou, Sesnick moved to New York to be nearer the group.

'There was quite a bit that went on prior to that decision being finalised. There were months of negotiations with various people acting as messengers betwen Lou and myself and the group, so there was quite a bit of time that was spent that spring and summer before it was settled.' *Steve Sesnick*

A 1967 tour of the States provided the Velvet Underground with the perfect opportunity to rehearse new material for their second album. But things didn't always run according to plan . . .

'One time, the Velvet Underground were playing at some airplane hanger out in LA.

It had been turned into something – you know, a multi-media experience for you and yours – and I was standing on the stage with Sterling and, all of a sudden, he says to me "Don't Move!" I take a look, and I'd just put on fresh strings, and one of the long ends had hit the microphone and just burned right up, and it was starting down the kneck of the guitar! Well, I didn't move. They shut everything down, and I just stood there, and there was smoke and that terrible ozone odour in the air. I mean, people get knocked out, killed. It's incredible. I mean, that kind of jolt cannot be doing good things to your system . . . I've always had a big fear of electric shocks.' *Lou Reed*

'We worked the Masonic Hall in Columbus,

ANDY WARHOL AT THE FACTORY.

Ohio. A huge place filled with people drinking and talking. Played a whole set to no applause, just silences.' *John Cale*

'Who can you talk to on the road? Long-haired dirty drug people wherever you look. The boy passes over a bag of green powder and passes out. Don't take that, it has horse tranquilliser in it. Oh, I shot up to your song. I got busted to your song. Oh please bless me and touch me and make it all go away. I loved to you.' *Lou Reed*

'God, you get out on the road into these

PROMO SHOT AT THE TIME OF THEIR FIRST ALBUM.

towns with one TV station. You get so sick for New York – you have to grab a copy of Vogue.' *Lou Reed*

'Everyone has turned the whole Velvet thing into much more than it ever was. Memories are like . . . fun. And on the one hand they would like to have it just stay there. And on the other hand they would like to say, "Well, he's uh . . . not developing." So you lose either way.' *Lou Reed*

2. Beginning to See the Light: 1967-1970

BY CHRISTMAS 1967, the Velvet Underground's second album, White Light/White Heat *(recorded in California and produced by Tom Wilson) was released. Any animosity with Warhol seems to have been bridged, because Warhol again provided the cover concept. The seventeen-minute 'Sister Ray' (recorded in one take) dominated the record. Although Nico was now absent from the line-up, there were still problems with personality clashes during the recording of the album – mainly due to Reed's uncompromising manner with the rest of the band. It's been suggested that Sesnick was already targeting the main songwriter towards a solo career, and that Reed was finding it difficult coming to terms with the attention.*

WHITE LIGHT/WHITE HEAT (Verve) THE VELVET UNDERGROUND

WHITE LIGHT/WHITE HEAT (1968), THE VELVET UNDERGROUND'S SECOND ALBUM.

'They were quick in the studio. To sum it all up, it did go very fast. I think it was done in three days of recording. They were very rapid. They were well prepared when they went in. And their method of recording was such that it could be done very quickly, and they believed in that particular manner at the time, and it just went real fast . . . I would say that Lou was beyond proficient. He was a master at understanding the time and reasons for things . . . We felt very positive, we thought the record was great. We certainly were shocked when radio stations didn't think it was so great. But we were used to that. We never had airplay then – it just didn't happen – so we didn't care about it.' *Steve Sesnick*

'Dealers who cater to the underground market will find this disc a hot seller, for the Velvet Underground (minus Nico) feature intriguing lyrics penned by two of the group, Lou Reed and Sterling Morrison. Though the words tend to be drowned out by the pulsating instrumentation, those not minding to cuddle up to the speakers will joy to narrative songs such as "The Gift", the story of a boy and a girl.' Billboard *album review, February 1968*

' "Sister Ray" was built around this story that I wrote about this scene of total debauchery and decay. I like to think of Sister Ray as a transvestite smack dealer. The situation is a bunch of drag queens taking some sailors home with them and shooting up on smack and having this orgy when the police appear. And when it came to putting the music to it, it just had to be spontaneous. We turned up to ten, flat out, leakage all over the place. That's it. [The record company] asked us what we were going to do. We said, "We were going to start." They said, "Who's playing the bass?"

We said, "There is no bass." They asked us when it ends. We didn't know. When it ends, is when it ends.' *Lou Reed*

'I love Lou, but he has what must be a fragmented personality. So you're never too sure under any conditions what you're going to have to deal with.' *Sterling Morrison*

'I think everybody has a number of personalities, just in themselves. It's not just people having different personalities. I mean, you wake up in the morning and say "Wonder which one of them is around today?" You find out which one and send him out. Fifteen minutes later someone else shows up. That's why if there's no-one left to talk to, you can listen to a couple of them talking in your head.' *Lou Reed*

'Lou was starting to act funny. He brought in this guy called Sesnick – who I thought was a real snake – to be our manager, and all this intrigue started to take place. Lou

SECOND VERSION OF WHITE LIGHT/WHITE HEAT WITH A MORE ACCESSIBLE COVER DESIGN.

THE VELVET UNDERGROUND PROMOTING THEIR SECOND ALBUM *WHITE LIGHT/WHITE HEAT* (1967).

was calling us "his band", while Sesnick was trying to get him to go solo. Maybe it was the drugs he was doing at the time. They certainly didn't help.' *John Cale*

Differences aside, the Velvet Underground came the closest they ever got to cracking the big time in October 1967. While Reed and Cale bickered among themselves, Sesnick was busily lining up a deal with Brian Epstein that would send the band on a massive promotional trek across Europe. Sadly for everyone concerned, Epstein tragically died prior to the contracts being signed.

'I just remember a real edge with Lou all the time. Ego-jealousy. Lou was definitely the star. Any guy that is out there singing is the star. It was hard for John because he was back-up star. He had so much charisma. He had the balance of the Velvet Underground charisma. Lou without John, it wouldn't have had the edge . . . The *sound* of the Velvet Underground was John.' *Betsey Johnson*

By early 1968 the relationship was so bad between Reed and Cale, that they were reportedly coming to blows on a regular basis. Tensions weren't eased by the need to go on the road to promote the record.

'Lou placed heavy emphasis on lyrics, while Cale and I were more interested in blasting the house down.' *Sterling Morrison*

By **JOSEPH MANCINI**
With JOSEPH FEUREY
and JAY LEVIN

Pop artist Andy Warhol fought for his life today after being gunned down in his own studio by a woman who had acted in one of his underground films

The artist - sculptor - film-maker underwent 5½ hours of surgery performed by a four-man team of doctors at Columbus Hospital late last

*Andy Warhol: Life and Times.
By Jerry Tallmer. Page 3.*

night and was given a "50-50 chance to live."

He remained in critical condition today and his chances for life had not improved.

At 7:30 last night, just three hours and 10 minutes after the shooting, Valeria Solanis, 28, a would-be writer-actress, walked up to a rookie policeman directing traffic in Times Sq. and surrendered.

She reached into her trench coat and handed Patrolman William Schmalix, 22, a .32 automatic and a .22 revolver. The .32 had been fired recently, police

Continued on Page 8

Pop artist-film maker Andy Warhol makes the scene at a recent Long Island discotheque party. Valeria Solanis, who surrendered to police after he was shot and critically wounded, is shown as she was booked last night.

Post Photos by Borer and Engel

AT THE TIME OF THE ATTEMPTED MURDER OF ANDY WARHOL BY VALERIE SOLANES, RELATIONS BETWEEN HIM AND LOU REED HAD ALREADY BROKEN DOWN.

'We were very distraught at the time. There was pressure building up – God knows from where – and were all getting very frustrated.' *John Cale*

'I don't remember any specific crack. [John] just wasn't with them. It seemed real logical to me. I just really supported him and thought that he ought to do his own music. It was really his music, and then Lou's music. It seemed like they went as far as they could go.' *Betsey Johnson*

In April John Cale married fashion designer Betsey Johnson. Betsey is reputed to have caused

a lot of friction in the band, no doubt contributing to the now inevitable split. Two months later Andy Warhol narrowly survived an assassination attempt when a jealous hanger-on from the Factory, Valerie Solanes, who felt Warhol was not giving her the attention she felt she deserved, walked into the Factory and shot him several times at short range. Although he lived, Warhol's health would always be fragile from this point on.

'I was with Lou. We were going down in an elevator in the Beverly Wilshire Hotel. In that particular hotel they put the morning papers on the floor of the elevator. We were both extremely shocked and startled when

**THE VELVETS AS SHOWN ON THE REVERSE OF THEIR
SECOND ALBUM.**

we looked down and saw the headlines.
Bobby Kennedy was shot a few days later
. . . We were both extremely upset. It also
struck us as very scarey, because apparently
Lou knew who the girl was who did it. So
we were upset for Andy, and I was upset
and concerned for Lou – that something like
that might happen to him some day. As a
manager who watches over those things, it
was a very serious shock.' *Steve Sesnick*

'I was scared to call [Warhol], and in the
end I did and he asked me, "Why didn't you
come?"' *Lou Reed*

*In August 1968, Reed called a band meeting,
without inviting John Cale. The agenda concerned the latter's removal from the band if, that
is, the band was to continue. Lou reportedly
believed their musical differences to be irreconcil-
able. Cale was still motivated by the need to
experiment, while Reed was already thinking
in slightly more commercial terms. Since there*

was really only room for one leader, the others eventually succumbed to Lou's persuasiveness, and Cale played his final gig with the band at the Boston Tea Party during September. A replacement was found in the form of bassist Doug Yule.

'Lou called and asked me to meet him at the Riviera Cafe in the West Village. When I got there Maureen was also present. Lou had called a meeting to announce that John was out of the band . . . I said that we were the band, that it was graven on the tablets. So then a long and bitter argument ensued, with much banging on tables, and finally Lou said, "You don't go for it? All right, the band is dissolved." Now I could say that it was more important to keep the band together than to worry about Cale, but that wasn't really what decided me. I just wanted to keep on doing it. So finally I weighed my self-interest against Cale's interests and sold John out.' *Sterling Morrison*

'I wasn't that shocked, because the tensions were there, and John was obviously not too happy. But I was real sad, and worried we wouldn't proceed.' *Mo Tucker*

'Lou and I eventually found the group too small for both of us, and so I left.' *John Cale*

John Cale would go on to produce, in the short-term, Nico's album Marble Index, *and the first recorded material from the Stooges. By the end of the decade, he and Betsey would be divorced.*

'I never lost a night's rest. Except with John. That was a very critical incident. And we felt badly about it, but there was nothing to be done to stop it.' *Steve Sesnick*

'I'd have to say that Lou bumped John because of jealousy. One friend said that Lou had always told him he wanted to be a solo star. Lou never confided that to us, but John and I always knew that he really wanted some kind of recognition apart from

NICO – FROM HER SECOND ALBUM SLEEVE.

the band.' *Sterling Morrison*

'I only hope that one day John [Cale] will be recognised as . . . the Beethoven or something of his day. He knows so much about music, he's such a great musician. He's completely mad – but that's because he's Welsh.' *Lou Reed*

The band's self-produced third album, simply titled The Velvet Underground, *was released in March 1969. Lou immediately made claims on a conceptual masterpiece, years ahead of its time. Later he described it as a complete synopsis of worldly sin.*

'The Velvet Underground takes a journey through musical psychedelia, low-keyed in the main, but a trip that should be interesting to a good number of listeners. The Velvet Underground composed, arranged and conducted all selections on the album. Vocally and instrumentally, the group creates an evocative, sensuous sound, and

the LP could pick up considerable sales.' *Cashbox Magazine*

'Cale's departure allowed Lou Reed's sensitive, meaningful side to hold sway. Why do you think "Pale Blue Eyes" happened on the third album, with Cale out of there? That's a song about Lou's old girlfriend in Syracuse. I said, "Lou, if I wrote a song like that I wouldn't make you play it." My position on the album was one of acquiescence.' *Sterling Morrison*

'I was working with Doug [Yule's] innocence . . . I'm sure he never understood a word of what he was singing. He doesn't know what it's about. I mean, I thought it was so cute . . . I adore people who are like that.' *Lou Reed*

'This song would follow this song because this has to do with this and this has to do with that, and this will answer that and then you've got this character who matches this character or offsets this character etc etc. And the third album was really the quintessence of that idea, because it started out with "Candy Says", where this girl asks all these questions. And then the next song is

THE VELVET UNDERGROUND, NOW FEATURING DOUG YULE (RIGHT) HAPPILY POSE FOR THE THIRD ALBUM, *THE VELVET UNDERGROUND* (1969).

"What Goes On" where this guy says, "Wow, you're asking me all these questions, you're driving me crazy, you're making me feel like I'm upside down." And the third thing they've decided that they're talking about is love, so he's going to give her an example of "Some Kinds Of Love", and he talks about how all kinds of love are the same as long as it's love, and that's what he says to her over and over and gives different examples of it. He's trying to reach her and she's like saying, 'I don't understand', y'know, but that's stated at the beginning. . . "Afterhours" was like a sum-up, like it was kind of the cap, the frosting on the cake as far as I was concerned. I mean it's a terribly sad song and I didn't sing it because I figured people wouldn't believe me if I sang it. But I knew Maureen for instance had a very innocent voice.' *Lou Reed*

Their record company, Verve, wasn't too impressed however, and seemed reluctant to offer any more advances since the album showed little sign of selling. In return, the Velvets were reluctant to offer much more material – aiming instead for a new deal somewhere else. In the meantime though, the band did write and record some new

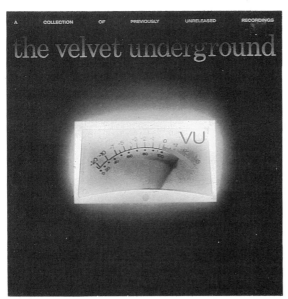

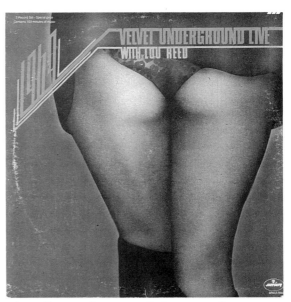

numbers – *which would be destined to emerge in 1985 on* VU, *the great 'lost' Velvet Underground album. They also embarked on a lot of live work in the months following Cale's departure, recordings of which would end up on the 1974 release –* Velvet Underground Live '69. *Sesnick lined up a new contract with Atlantic, but the ensuing* Loaded *album, released in September 1970, seemed half-baked and half-hearted, lacking the punch of their previous efforts. It was produced by the band themselves, with assistance from Geoffrey Haslam and Shel Kagan. With the pregnant Tucker replaced on drums by Yule's brother Billy, and Lou handing over much of the the vocal responsibilities to Doug, the record didn't deliver as much as Reed promised – even though it did include 'Sweet Jane' and 'Rock'n'Roll'!*

'I originally intended to do almost all the vocals on *Loaded*, but I blew my voice out at Max's, so Doug took over on several of them, and the sense that the songs were handled and interpreted in got changed – like "New Age" was supposed to be funny, a girl thinking she was like a movie queen and the guy down the block was Robert Mitchum. And "Sweet Nuthin'" was even more different – it was intended as a rather sly song making fun of some people that it

describes and not at all the sort of very serious statement it ultimately became.' *Lou Reed*

Lou has always seemed very bitter about the final outcome of the album.

'The songs are out of order, they don't form a cohesive unit, they just leap about. They don't make sense thematically. The end of "Sweet Jane" was cut off, the end of "New

Age" was cut off, the guitar solo on "Train Coming Round The Bend" was fucked around with and inserted.' *Lou Reed*

'They did some editing. On "Sweet Jane" towards the ending, it had a minor melody which was so pretty . . . it made sense, but they edited it out. That was sheer stupidity, blatant stupidity. On "New Age" it goes, "Something's got a hold on me and I don't know what . . . it's the beginning of a new age . . ." That was supposed to go on for a full minute, that was the powerful part of the song, they have it go for one chorus!

How could anyone be that stupid? They took all the power out of those songs.' *Lou Reed*

'I just gave up on it. I wasn't there when it was done.' *Lou Reed*

'I wasn't there to put the songs in order. If I could have stood it, I would have stayed there and showed them what to do.' *Lou Reed*

A 1970 COLLAGE FROM THE LONDON-BASED RADICAL NEWSPAPER *FRIENDS*, WHICH FEATURED A LESS THAN COMPLIMENTARY FIRST-HAND DESCRIPTION OF THE LATTERDAY VELVETS' MAX'S RESIDENCY.

His relationship with Sesnick becoming increasingly strained, Reed enjoyed a final fling at Max's Kansas City in the summer of 1970. Although the shows were generally shambolic, the final night of the run – Sunday 23 August – was a scorcher. Recorded for posterity by Warhol's friend Brigid Polk, and subsequently released by Atlantic in May 1972 as the Live At Max's Kansas City *album, the show provided a significant watershed in Lou Reed's career. Although no-one knew it then, it would be his final performance with the Velvet Underground for more than twenty years.*

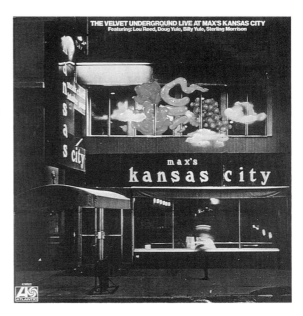

'I hated those last bookings at Max's . . . because I couldn't do the songs I wanted to do, and I was under a lot of pressure to do things I didn't want to – and it finally reached a crescendo. I never in my life thought I would not do what I believed in and there I was, not doing what I believed in, that's all, and it made me sick. It dawned on me that I'm doing what somebody else is telling me to do supposedly for my own good, because they're supposed to be so smart. But only one person can write it, and that person should know what it's about. I'm not a machine that gets up there and parrots off these songs. And standing around the bar – you don't have to get high to get into me. I have made it a point not to be oblique. And I was giving out interviews at the time saying yes, I wanted the group to be a dance band, I wanted to do that, but there was a large part of me that wanted to do something else. I was talking as if I were programmed.'

Lou's sense of paranoia during this period seems to have got the better of him, as well as everyone else around him. The fact that he is said to have been having just six hours sleep a week, probably didn't help. But the indications are that a solo career was very much in his mind.

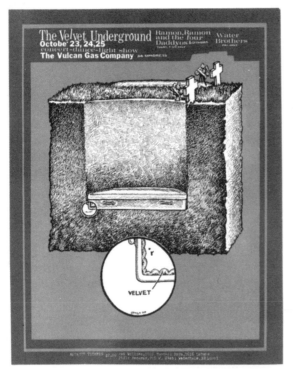

'We were always anti-performers, and Lou was leaping around doing all those gestures he does now. I didn't realise it until Lou told me that later on. But Sesnick had often exhorted us all to be more dynamic on stage, and I guess he had been working on Lou in particular.' *Sterling Morrison*

VELVET UNDERGROUND & CHARLEY MUSSELWHITE & INITIAL SHOCK
Lights By Jerry Abrams Headlights
friday-saturday-sunday
OCTOBER 18-19-20

SUTTER AT VAN NESS
in san francisco
AVALON BALLROOM

THE DYING THROES OF THE VELVET UNDERGROUND, RECORDED FOR POSTERITY ON POSTERS AND ALBUMS.

'That part of me that wanted to do something else wasn't allowed to express itself, in fact it was being cancelled out. And it turned out that that was the part that made up 90 per cent of Lou. There was that comment by that guy that I became unplugged from objective reality, and got very sick at what I saw, what I was doing to myself. I didn't belong there. I didn't want to be a mass pop national hit group with followers. I don't want that. If it happens to them, more power to them, I hope they have a lot of fun, but I didn't want that. I knew we could do the high-energy rock and everybody can dance. That's OK. But the last night I was there, when Brigid made her tape, that was the only night I really enjoyed myself. I did all the songs I wanted – a lot of them were ballads. High-energy does not necessarily mean fast. High-energy has to do with heart.' *Lou Reed*

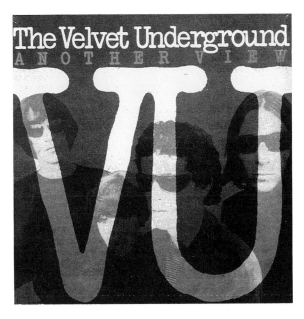

c/o The Velvet Underground
New York, N.Y.

Robert Greenfield

Roswell Angier

The Velvet Underground could have closed out their career as the aging darlings of the avant-garde. Instead, they released a third LP studded with prayerful diamonds of song, invoked Jesus, saw the light, dispelled the shades of heroin and speed. Then they toured around the country, where new songs matched old, though new images took longer replacing the old and dying ones. The transition from demonic/divine to human takes a while. Currently, The Velvet Underground possesses all the qualities of a fine breed car, a Lotus, let's say--well-tooled, almost-mean, the lines elegant, tasteful, impressive but, miraculously, not beyond the means of the average consumer. The whole thing functions with a simplicity of motion which indicates careful, affectionate construction and a refinement of basic design. The combustion, once noisy and visible, is now internal and implicit. The current pop vernacular is dense, complicated, thick with musical commonplace and lyric cliche. The Underground is lean, direct and anything but dated.

'Lou was relying totally on Sesnick, but Sesnick felt Lou was too hard to handle and finally told him, "I don't care if you live or die." Lou couldn't face this. It was like a hard divorce, to be very sudenly slapped in the face by someone you trusted. One night I'm sitting in a booth upstairs at Max's eating a cheeseburger, and Lou comes up and says, "Sterling, I'd like you to meet my parents." I was astonished. Lou always had an extremely troubled relationship with his parents. They hated the fact that Lou was playing music and hanging around with undesirables. I was always afraid of Lou's parents. There was this constant threat of them seizing Lou and having him thrown into the nuthouse. That was always over our heads. Every time that Lou got hepatitis, his parents were waiting to seize him and lock him up. So I was thinking, "What in the world can this portend?"' *Sterling Morrison*

'There were a lot of things going on that summer. Internally, within the band, the situation, the milieu, and especially the management. Situations which could only be solved by as abrupt a departure as possible, once I had made the decision. I just walked out, because we didn't have any money, I didn't want to tour again – I can't get any writing done on tour, and the grind is terrible – and I've wondered for a long time if we were ever going to be accepted on a large scale. Words can't do justice to the way I got worked over with the money. But I'm not a businessman. I've always said, "I don't care about it," and generally I've gotten fucked as a result of that attitude.' *Lou Reed*

'The music is all. People should die for it. People are dying for everything else, so why not the music?' *Lou Reed*

'If it wasn't me, I would have idolised myself in the Velvets. I loved what we did and I'm proud of it. We stood for everything that kids loved and adults hated. We were loud, you couldn't understand the lyrics, we were vulgar, we sang about dope, sex violence – you name it. It wasn't the nocturnal side of rock'n'roll, it was the daylight side, no-one else had noticed it that's all. It didn't take any nerve to write those songs. We didn't have to fight anyone to have them recorded. I mean the record company didn't know what we were doing, they couldn't stand listening to our records, really. All they knew is that we sold just enough albums to justify making another one, and that other groups were being signed up and they were citing us as an influence. Christ knows why, we didn't know what we were doing. When they first let the Velvets out of the bag, we couldn't understand the reaction, we didn't know why everyone was reeling in shock. Nobody told us what we were doing to cause such a reaction. I mean, I've said to Andy [Warhol] since, "Why didn't you tell us?"' *Lou Reed*

'They were graphic songs, to this day "Heroin" is a graphic song, and that song works in any context. No matter what you do you can't butcher that song. Y'know, I'd really love to hear Frank Sinatra do it, really. It would be just incredible to hear Frank Sinatra coming out with that song on some middle-of-the-road radio station, because that song doesn't mince words, neither did the Velvets.' *Lou Reed*

'The real thing is not something that you'd want to idolise . . . If you play the albums chronologically it covers the growth of us as people from here to there, and in there is a tale for everybody in case they want to know what you can do to survive the scenes. If you line the songs up and play them, you should be able to relate and not feel alone. I think it's important that people don't feel alone.' *Lou Reed*

'It was a process of elimination from the start. First no more Andy, then no more Nico, then no more John, then no more Velvet Underground.' *Lou Reed*

THE VELVET Underground (consisting of Morrison, Tucker, Yule and Walter Powers – an associate of Sesnick's from Boston) staggered on without Reed (even playing in Britain) till they finally sank without trace. Their last album Squeeze, *in 1973, featuring Doug Yule's pale imitation of Lou Reed, was treated with universal contempt. Meanwhile Lou took a break from the music business, went back to live with his parents in Freeport, Long Island, and took a job with his father's company – while simultaneously sorting out the legal difficulties associated with his contractual attachment to Atlantic. And there it could all have ended if it hadn't been for David Bowie who, during his rise to fame in 1971, began to speak of Reed's influence on his own work. The British star's interest in the cult New Yorker inevitably spawned renewed record company interest in Reed.*

'I was a typist for two years in the family business. My mother always told me in high school, "You should take typing, it gives you something to fall back on." She was right.' *Lou Reed*

'I'm not going to do things that are complicated anymore, because I realised that people just don't catch it, and now I'm not that excited by the idea.' *Lou Reed*

Instead Lou concentrated on more simple compositions, of personal experience.

'I'm very good at the glib remark that may not mean something if you examine it too closely, but it still sounds great.' *Lou Reed*

'I'm always studying people that I know, and when I think I've got them worked out, then I go away and write a song about them. When I sing that song I become them. It's for that reason that I'm kind of empty when I'm not doing anything. I don't have a personality of my own, I just pick up on other people's.' *Lou Reed*

'Lou has been a powerful influence on a host of contemporary performers . . . myself included.' *David Bowie*

Lou turned to friends for support and encouragement with his new work. And it was three of his closest, Lisa Robinson (the writer), her husband

Lou Reed makes his mark.
Lou Reed, supermusician and legendary city poet. On his own now, with a new album "Lou Reed" LSP-4701.
Songs and secrets from the phantom of rock.

RC/ Records and Tapes

Richard, and Danny Fields, who were able to put him in contact with Dennis Katz, the head of A&R at RCA Records. The introduction proved invaluable and, following a subsequent deal with RCA, May 1972 saw the release of Lou Reed's eponymously titled debut album as a solo artist. Recorded at London's Morgan Studios, Lou co-produced the LP with Richard Robinson. Interestingly the session musicians included guitarist Steve Howe and keyboard player Rick Wakeman (the latter also appeared on Bowie's Space Oddity album during the same period), both of whom were on their way to international stardom as part of the English rock band Yes. Feeling confident enough to renew old acquaintances, Lou met up with John Cale and Nico (who had continued to collaborate with each other since the demise of the Velvet Underground) while on a visit to Paris, and even played with them on a few numbers. Their past problems seemed, for the time being, to be water under the bridge.

I always wanted to do a song like "Berlin", the Barbra Streisand thing, a real night club torch song. If you were Frank Sinatra you'd loosen your tie and light a cigarette.' *Lou Reed, following his visit to Paris*

Lou Reed
RCA 4701

Well, Lou Reed's first statement since his emergence from the underground is here, and it's good. it's great, even. I've got some complaints (critics sound dumb without at least a couple of gripes and grumbles), but I'll tell you right now that most of them concern the areas in which Lou's solo music differs from the stuff he did with The Velvet Underground, that mythic band of lovely down-heads which was (is) the darling of the rock press and one of my personal all-time favorites. The only fault that belongs entirely to this set lies in some of the performances by Lou. He has been singing a lot of these songs for quite a while, going back to the Velvets days, and I've seen him just plain *sing* a lot of 'em better. Even so, his vocals are consistently vivid and compelling.

But the main thing that keeps me from going totally ga-ga over this album is (I hestitate to say it) its overwhelming cleanliness. It was obvious when Lou took off for merry old England in search of some polished session men ("They're not payed to think, just play"—Ray Davies), that this was not going to be a typical velvety chunky under-ground-sounding album. But I figured that Lou knew what he was looking for and I certainly have enough faith in his taste to give him the benefit of the doubt. But now I just don't know. The musicians on this session are simply not as sympathetic towards Lou's great lyrics as The Velvets were. So even though we have the most expertly produced (by Lou and Richard Robinson) album in Reed's career (complete with great cover art by Tom Adams, who is responsible for the fantastic paperback covers of Raymond Chandler's equally fantastic mysteries), it seems like something was definitely sacrificed along the way. I mean these guys (Caleb Quaye, Rick Wakeman, Steve Howe, and Paul Keogh, to name some) are good, but they are strictly back-up. Very clean and very distant.

The best example of what I'm talking about is the opening cut, "I Can't Stand It." Here's a song that woulda been great on any Velvets record, and they make it sound like they're havin' a tough time just mustering up enough energy to keep the fast pace. Plus Lou's vocals on the choruses are all but obliterated by a couple of sweeties who seem to have learned their trade from the Leon Russell School for Aspiring Female Back-ground Vocalists.

OK, I've gone on long enough like this; the songs here are generally A-1 Super-Fine. My favorites are "Wild Child," the story of a female street hippie, in which Lou describes a conversation:

> I was talking to Chuck in his Genghis
>   Khan suit and his wizard's hat
> He spoke of his movie and how he was
>   makin' a new soundtrack
> And then we spoke of kids on the Coast
> And different types of organic soap
> And the way suicides don't leave notes
> Then we spoke of Lorraine
> Always back to Lorraine . . .
> She's a wild child. . . .

"Berlin," a sentimental journey to a dimly lit cafe taken to mourn a recently past love affair; and "Lisa Says," in which some really nice lady helps the singer to overcome his shyness.

So make no mistake, there is a lot to Lou Reed and his first solo album. In fact, the more I suppress my desire to hear these songs done by The Velvet Underground, it becomes one of the best albums of this not-so-new-any-more year.

Gary Kenton

LOU RE-UNITES WITH JOHN CALE AND NICO, PLAYING AN ACOUSTIC SET AT THE BATACLAN IN PARIS, 1972.

Lou was being managed during the recording of the album by Fred Heller, who had been recommended by Dennis Katz, but during the following US promotional tour, Katz took over the role himself. With Katz's keen eye for promotion, and his vast array of contacts to call on, Lou was invited to appear with David Bowie at London's Royal Festival Hall – as part of a benefit concert for a Save The Whales charity. By the time Lou opened his UK tour a week later, with his backing band, the Tots, Bowie's debt of influence had been repayed, with Lou swaggering onto the stage in glitter and eye-liner.

'I did three or four shows like that, then it was back to leather. We were just kidding around – I'm not into make-up.' *Lou Reed*

'My first album's got a song called "I love You" on it. I always wanted to write a song

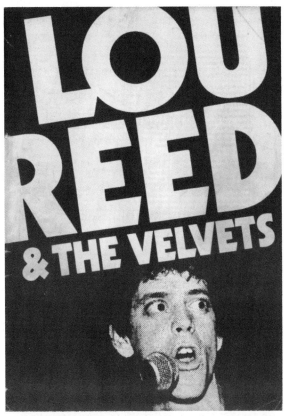

NIGEL TREVENA'S INDISPENSABLE BOOKLET OF
1973 WAS VIRTUALLY THE ONLY SOURCE OF FACTS TO BE
FOUND ABOUT THE VELVETS AT THAT TIME.

called "I Love You" and make it fresh. I figured if I could take a phrase like that and turn it into something, then that would be something of an accomplishment.' *Lou Reed*

'As far as I'm concerned it's the album we need most of all right now, the one which takes us above and beyond all the superstar crap and back into music. Or forward into music, because I don't want to say this is a "back to the roots" album. It's just that listening to it gives me the kind of charge I haven't had in God knows how long.' *Richard Williams, talking about* Lou Reed *in the Melody Maker*

'It's a great deal of fun for me to do a lyric like "Love makes you feel ten feet tall", or

51

Lester Bangs spends a Perfect Day with Lou Reed

YOU WALK into the dining room of the Holiday Inn filled with expectation at finally getting to meet one of the musical and psychological frontiersmen of our time. Lou Reed, who with his group the Velvet Underground was singing about dragqueens and heroin at least five years before such obsessions reached the mass level. Who began a comeback as a solo artist last summer in England, and under the wing of David Bowie produced *Transformer*, a classic of mondo bendo rock. Who then, having come out of the closet at last, returned to his New York home and ushered ... ...ting married to an actress ... named Betty (stage

... ...er and ...ou ...e

bathtub and started fingering the Dippity Do jar."

Everything is yoks to this bibulous bozo; he really makes a point of havin' some fun! Although it does disturb his friends and fans to see him in such failing health. But he can find a joke even there. At one point I asked him when he intended to die.

"I would like would like to live to a ripe old age and raise watermelons in Wyoming."

Then he takes another glug and machos: "I'm outdrinking you two to one, you know."

"Are you proud of yourself?"

"Yeah. No, not actually; it's just that a single shot of Scotch is so small that you've gotta nurse it like it's a child or something. I drink constantly."

"How does it treat your nervous system?" I probed.

"It destroys it," he beamed.

"Then how do you intend to raise your watermelons?"

"Well, my time will come. By now I'm getting tired of liquor because there's just nothing strong enough. Now if we were ...king 150 proof sake, or something like

if in any way my album helps people decide who or what they are, then I will feel I have accomplished something in my life. But I don't feel that way at all. I don't think an album's gonna do anything. You can't listen to a record and say, 'Oh that really turned me onto gay life, I'm gonna be gay.' A lot of people will have one or two experiences, and that'll be it. Things may not change one iota. It's beyond the control of a straight person to turn gay at the age he'll probably be listening to any of his stuff or reading about it; he'll already be determined psychologically. It's like Franco said: 'Give me a child until he's seven and he's mine.' By the time a kid reaches puberty they've been determined. Guys walking around in makeup is just fun. Why shouldn't men be able to put on makeup and have fun like women have?'

Lou Reed just may have a better perspective on this supposed upheaval in sexual roles than any of these Gore Vidals and Jill Johnstons. Duds comin' outa the closet in droves and finding out they're heterosexual! Ha! Only trouble is that Lou's

"I found a reason for living, and the reason dear is you". People say "Oh man, it's Lou Reed it must be a put on", well they're wrong. I love that stuff, always have, always will. It's hopeless, there's nothing to be done about it. I'll listen to that stuff till they put me away.' *Lou Reed*

' "Ocean" evokes the ocean in a fairly unpleasant manner. A guy goes mad on the track, the ocean engulfs him. The person on that track is one example of a mad person in a mad situation . . . like a lot of my friends are mad, but aren't we all. Who isn't, especially in cities, my God.' *Lou Reed*

Lou entered Trident Studios, London, during August 1972 to record the Transformer *album. David Bowie and Mick Ronson, fresh from their success with the* Ziggy Stardust *album, joined him as producers – and players. Their involvement clearly gave Reed the confidence and support to create an album which would reflect the mood of bisexual revolution that was taking place.*

'Mick Ronson plays in exactly the style I want – upfront.' *Lou Reed*

'The people I was around at the time thought

ABOVE: A RATHER BLOATED PHANTOM OF ROCK IN ACTION (1973).

Bowie would be the perfect producer for me to make a record that would sell. And it turned out to be totally true, didn't it?' *Lou Reed*

'There's a lot of sexual ambiguity on the album, and two outright gay songs – from me to them, but carefully worded so the straights can miss out on the implications and enjoy them without being offended.' *Lou Reed*

'If I was to retire now, "Walk On The Wild Side" is the one I'd want to be known by. That's my masterpiece. That's the one that'll make them forget "Heroin".' *Lou Reed*

'I liked "Walk On The Wild Side". I found the secret with that one. I was supposed to write a play called *The Walk On The Wild Side* and I read the book [by Nelson Algren] and wrote the song. Nothing came of the play, but I wasn't going to waste the time and energy I put into the song – so I put it out.' *Lou Reed*

'Any song that mentions oral sex, male prostitution, methedrine, valium and still gets Radio 1 airplay, must be truly cool.' *Nick Kent, New Musical Express*

' "Andy's Chest" is about Andy Warhol being shot by Valerie Solanes, even though the lyrics don't sound anything like that.' *Lou Reed*

'And then there's "Vicious" . . . The thing

ABOVE: FLYER FOR 'VICIOUS'. RIGHT: ON TOUR WITH THE TOTS (1972).

about this album is that all the songs are hate songs. My first solo album was all love songs – this is all hate songs.' *Lou Reed*

'*Transformer* has a cover you just won't believe. The back has a photo of this big

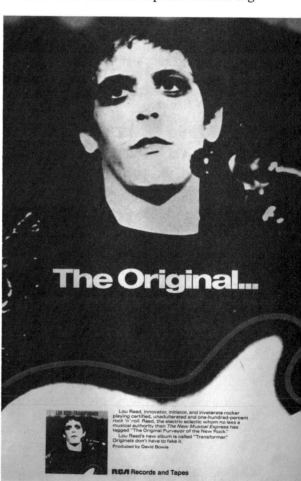

The Original...

Lou Reed, innovator, initiator, and inveterate rocker playing certified, unadulterated and one-hundred-percent *rock 'n' roll.* Reed, the electric eclectic whom no less a musical authority than *The New Musical Express* has tagged "The Original Purveyor of the New Rock."

Lou Reed's new album is called "Transformer." Originals don't have to fake it.

Produced by David Bowie

RCA Records and Tapes

well-hung stud looking into the mirror, and this sylph-like forties female creature staring out at him. The front cover is the most beautiful face in the world – mine.' *Lou Reed*

'*Transformer* is more like what the third Velvet Underground album would have sounded like if David Bowie had been in production back then . . . there's something especially fine about it which sets it apart from all the other crappy platters being released lately. I mean, hell, at least it ain't anal retentive.' *Robert A. Hull, Creem*

'When he's not being troubled by things around him, Lou's a very generous person, with time and conversation.' *David Bowie*

'David Bowie's very clever. We found we had a lot of things in common. He learned how to be hip. Associating with me brought his name out to a lot more people. He's very good in the studio. In a manner of speaking he produced an album for me.' *Lou Reed*

'David's wicked really. You know he told me that "Rock'n'Roll Suicide" was written for me.' *Lou, recalling the Bowie composition from the classic* Ziggy Stardust *album.*

'I love David Bowie, he's got everything. The kid's got everything . . . *everything*.' *Lou Reed*

'There's only one person with a viler temper than mine, and that's David Bowie.' *Lou Reed*

'Alice Cooper really doesn't make it as a drag queen. I mean he's so ugly. Iggy [Pop], now Iggy's really very beautiful, and so's David, but Alice! . . .' *Lou Reed*

'You can't fake being gay. If they claim they're gay, they're going to have to make love in a gay style, and most people aren't capable of making that commitment. That line that everyone's bisexual – I think that's just meaningless.' *Lou Reed*

THE UNHOLY TRINITY: (L. TO R.:) DAVID BOWIE, IGGY POP AND LOU REED (1973).

LOU REED'S IMAGE STRAIGHTENED OUT SOMEWHA[T]
THE TIME OF HIS MARRIAGE TO BETTY KRONSTADT[,]
1973. THEY SPLIT BEFORE THE END OF THE YEAR.

LOU REED HAS ALWAYS MADE GOOD CARTOON FODDER.
EARLY SEVENTIES UNDERGROUND COMIC,
WITH GROSSLY ALTERED LYRICS TO GLAM ROCK HITS OF
THE TIME.

'What I was writing about with the Velvet Underground was just what was going on around me. I didn't realise it was a whole new world for everybody else. Everybody else is now at the point where I was at in 1967. Makes me wonder where they'll be at in five years time. Come to that, it makes me wonder where I'm at now!' *Lou Reed*

'I never mean what I say . . . I never keep to things unless I actually promise. I told some journalist that I was very hung up on cowboys. If I saw him today I'd probably tell him I was really aggressive and that all cowboys are a bunch of assholes. I'm really very inconsistent.' *Lou Reed*

Increasingly irritated by the role-model tag being pinned to rock stars, Lou took a stand against any such personal representation in his work – and in its promotion.

'I was being tutored that I could be an example of this, of that, how someone could move from drugs to spirituality, but I don't want to be an example of anything. I don't think that people can be examples of anything very much to anybody else, outside of being nice, and all the obvious things. Don't steal, don't cut your neighbour's toes off, we all know that. I don't like to be told what to do, or tell anyone else what to do. Like drugs – I think drugs are terrible, for me. I also personally feel they're terrible for a lot of other people, but that's for them to go fool around in and figure out. If someone asked, "Lou, what do you think of drugs?" I'd say, "Lou thinks they're monumentally awful, and I'm glad I lived through it." And if someone wants to take it from there I think they could figure out that maybe I didn't think drugs were a great idea. I write better when I'm eating health foods, when I'm with someone I like. You do a lot of terrible things to your ego if you lean on things that are put together by pharmacists, because they don't have your best interests in mind, they just want the money. Being

59

DEGENERATE REGENERATION

Lou Reed's

By Tim Ferris
Photographs
By Andy Warhol

with people I really like is much better for me. The way it was going for a while, I thought I might end up appearing onstage in spangles and beads. I'd rather wear a sports coat.' *Lou Reed*

'The only way to go through something is to go right into the middle, the only way to do it is to not kid around. Storm coming, you go right through the centre and you may come out alright. Most people don't even know there is a centre. What you have to worry about is insanity. All the people I've known who were fabulous have either died or flipped, or gone to India. Either that or they've concentrated on one focal point, which is what I'm doing.' *Lou Reed*

'You know, if God showed up tomorrow and said what do you want to do, yeah, if he said – Do you want to be President? No. Do you want to be in politics? No. Do you want to be a lawyer? No. What do you want? I want to be a rhythm guitar player.' *Lou Reed*

'I think a lot of my music is about growing up in a way. It's nice to be mature, to be

able to meet things rationally sometimes, instead of with all this nervous sort of emotionalism.' *Lou Reed*

Following an American tour early in 1973, again with the Tots, Lou married Betty Kronstadt, reversing the image of homosexual perversity that had accompanied his association with David Bowie at the time Transformer *was released. Betty was a part-time waitress and would-be actress who he'd known since his period of semi-retirement. They'd apparently met in a super-market and, although publicly she seemed to be keeping Lou's feet on the ground, privately the rising star was having a hard time finding them.*

'When I get bored, funny things happen.' Lou Reed

'I drink constantly. It destroys the nervous system. I'm getting tired of liquor because there's just nothing strong enough.' *Lou Reed*

'I still do shoot speed, my doctor gives it to me. Well no, actually, they're just shots of meth mixed with vitamins . . .' *Lou Reed*

As 'Walk On The Wild Side' eventually proved successful in the UK as a single (it finally climbed to no.10 – seven months after its release), a British tour was lined up for the summer of 1973, though this was delayed slightly to allow Reed time to record his new album, Berlin.

'I enjoyed those shows I did in London at the Rainbow, but I kept thinking that Frank Zappa fell seventeen feet down into that pit. I hate Frank Zappa, and it made me so happy to think about that.' *Lou Reed*

'Frank Zappa is probably the single most untalented person I've heard in my life. He's two-bit, pretentious, academic, and he can't play his way out of anything. He can't play rock'n'roll because he's a loser. And that's why he dresses up funny. He's not happy with himself, and I think he's right.' *Lou Reed*

BY all accounts, Lou Reed had been Hard at Work. The quiet American had been keeping himself to himself: his nights in the studio, his days asleep at the Inn on the Park, and it was an owl-eyed Reed who finally emerged on Monday night — his first day off since his arrival to record a new album — to talk to us.

I had actually bumped into him once already during his visit, when he had showed his head at David Bowie's party and was photographed cheek-by-jowl with his old friend the host and elder statesman Mick Jagger, but he was in no mood for anything but light banter and the passing remark that he didn't think they invited journalists to this sort of thing. But dear boy, this is London, not New York.

Anyway, Lou Reed is far from the disphonously-suited dilettante that he pretended to be. After the party, hard though it may have been, he forced himself back, in the grey light of dawn, to Morgan Studios in Willesden to see how the chaps had been getting on in his absence. In no fit state, let it be said, for him to make any active contribution, but they had been working on something for which they did not need his assistance: "They told me to go to the party and come back with fresh ears. They couldn't hear it any more because they'd heard it so many times."

Reed's name has certainly spread abroad since the first occasion he arrived in London, known only to a few who had followed the career of the Velvet Underground to its unseemly conclusion. Here he became known as something of a prophet unhonoured in his own land, and soon his live shows with the Tots (this on his second visit) picked up quite a lively and vociferous following.

Reed was obliging enough to return "Heroin" to pride of place in his set, although he had unequivocally stated (on the official bootleg from Max's Kansas City, his former stomping ground) that he did not do the song any more. He made a dent on the British charts with his superb single "Walk On The Wild Side", titled after a Fifties movie, which spread far and wide and eventually even washed up at Reed's home shores, where it also crept into the charts.

In fact only the other Sunday I was walking through Denham, Bucks, the ...

OWL EYED IN BERLIN

fasting lightly ...

... with the simple ... it ...

REED'S RAINBOW

LOU REED at the Rainbow — for two nights. That will be the climax to his European tour which starts at the Melody Maker's Crystal Palace Garden Party on Saturday.

The two dates, at the London venue, on October 5 and 6, have been the subject of much speculation since the tour was only this week, however, that they were officially confirmed.

Reed will be bringing with him a new backing band consisting of Prakash John (bass), Richard Wagner and Steve Hunter (guitars), Ray Colcord (keyboards) and Pentti Whitey Glan (drums).

The band has only been with Reed for the past two weeks, following the demise of his previous backing group. June saw them played city two weeks together.

Both guitarists have done work with Alice Cooper and Wagner work with Detroit band called Frost. Glan was formerly with Canadian band, Mandala. Colcord was with Sky Train. Bob Ezrin was previously a producer with Nimbus9 records.

In addition, Wagner played lead on Reed's forthcoming album Berlin, released in September. The album was produced by Ezrin with Aynsley Dunbar among London with Aynsley Dunbar, Jack Bruce and Steve Winwood among the session musicians.

Also on the bill throughout the tour will be the acoustic group, the Persuasions.

After the MM Crystal Palace Garden Party concert, Reed continues on the Continent until September 21. The album has a date at the Apollo, when he has a date at the Apollo, Glasgow.

Other dates include Manchester (25), Southampton (26), Leicester (28), Sheffield (29), Newcastle (3), and Birmingham (October 3), and Birmingham Rainbow concerts will be available from the Saturday Garden Party programme: page 15.

point of view and his point of view is not particularly pleasant. Everything's seen from him."

Why the appeal of Berlin which, it transpires, Reed has never visited? "It represents certain things to me. It's a divided city and a lot of potentially violent things go on there. And it's not America, although some of the characters would appear to be American. It seemed better than calling it 'Omaha'. Berlin was just suggestive to me. To me it was a very good place to locate the scene of action. It makes it tastier that it's in Berlin — it reminds me of von Stroheim and Dietrich."

... seemed an appropriate ... to detail my own experiences of Berlin and to ... novelist Gunter Grass's ... ks about Berlin being ... nly place for twentieth ... y man to live in, being ... nd in alien territory — ... nt image of alienation ... hizophrenia. Reed was ... that it excited such ... ces but when I cast ... n whether such things ... mean much to the ... record buyer, he ... ed that "To most ... rlin is Germany, and ... his World War I and ... ar II — you don't ... a mental giant to ... out. But the more ... d you are the more ... resents."

INTERVI...

4. Animal Lou: 1973-1975

WHEN LOU announced he would be working with producer Bob Ezrin, the man who helped Alice Cooper achieve commercial success, the rock world anticipated an upbeat, mainstream-style record. Instead, it got an album described by Martin Kirkup in Sounds *as 'Probably the most depressing album of the decade.' The album was* Berlin. *Recorded at London's Morgan Studios and New York's Record Plant in the summer of 1973, musicians included Steve Hunter and Dick Wagner on guitars, Steve Winwood (and Ezrin himself) on keyboards, Aynsley Dunbar on drums, and Jack Bruce and Tony Levin on bass.*

'Everybody said, "Don't do it Lou, you're asking for it." So we did it, and the results have been very strange.'
Lou Reed

'*Berlin* is just very straightforward, and real. The lyrics are very direct, very to the point. It is a realistic story, y'know. It isn't just Berlin, it could be New York too.' *Lou Reed*

Lou hadn't actually visited Berlin during this period, but liked the symbolism of the city as a title. He presumably felt it reflected the subject matter of the album – a story of two people having a destructive relationship, closely based on the ones in his own life.

'Berlin is a divided city [in 1973], and a lot of potentially violent things go on there.. And it's not America, though some of the characters appear to be American. It just

RIGHT: LOU REED HAD ACHIEVED THE STATUS OF LEGEND AS EARLY AS 1973.

"I Just Don't Care At All"

"WHY DON'T you simply and write a word?" Still Lou Reed blithely halfway through the mammoth eight hour session from which this piece emerges.

Thankfully, it was a suggestion and not an easy, but it's clear that if a British thing to be cherished in nothing more than a love for reviews. And when asked why, he merely gives a non-committal shrug of the shoulders.

In fact, this particular reading was set so much on interview as just petitioning with the man in his hotel. During the course of the conversation, Lou's sardonic run the game from outright elation to sheer misery and halfway back again.

In several seven o'clock and we long back to his London base I am. A knowingly following the previous evening, Lou was to be found stashed out on his bed convincing. He's I most capable of sheer horror at incredible energy, which then seems to have completely drained, at this moment in time he was feeling very hot for from the first half hour spoke in a severely detestable snide.

He picks up a paper to read some-

thing that has been written about him and and finding it in his blazing motion suffer against its rather thin things the paper resorts to any but read them come service too drinks.

He has lost a lot of weight since I first saw him. Referring "I'm too far the too weight seem to actually be hard to figure out how to give up in the first place too, though he drinks nothing more than a few for its reviews. And how the day be going out to failure, he never seems to eat any thing.

The drinks arrive and a few sips do his vein the world of good. He set up on and begin the least gently upright. In a corner of the room there a second player with a copy of his new album, "Berlin" on the turntable. At last thing I feel only heard through a nation and was mercies to hear the final piece. I asked if I might put it on.

"If you like," says Lou without any enthusiasm.

Aren't you pleased with it, Lou?

"Yes, I hear each and every note of it, but I'm not sure I want to hear it." However by the time it started to play it's questionably "Why do you make me describing me to your place as I look?" but at last as you see." Certainly, to try, plotting shows, and shouting slightly to

raising his back off the ground, he does not affort make die from.

Most Names, the superb had gathered in Lou's hotel room, to and asks Lou to play him "Berlin." He played on the album, has hasn't heard the played on the album, and if of Simon's language, with whom Lou's became from Britain, address to since him up. The time of getting on a wave of London hare is assured and reacts on with the film. He completely Lou an itinerant portray in as it it Lou wants to are the exit, however if not there'd like to go out to it.

Kindly rebutching my saving he arrives phone to go with him then to go about and you it, and to they go and he stays put. Apart from each new of blindness, he's the perfect gentleman, articulating the messenger the truth, seguents the this experience which happens to slag by for a few words.

Somehow, once surrounded by the friends. Lou seems a way lonely person he's said to sofa quite tender in his lonely apart and clean she is now living in their New York homes, it's likely that his return will be as an heard. Ask him if he is bandy through his life anyway. "So on my son and I'd happier that way," but his ages have a real, however then it are truly bleeds ago.

But perhaps too spirits, he says that the is far more fun then doing it found interior in a raised come piece often, tapering, I reminds him of how, in a real sword at our early interview grants my absolutely impossible to talk to. Laughing he proclaims "There's only one person who has a very anyone the was and Pol c David Bowie."

That's least fair enough for some thing about you.

He who?" exclaims Lou in mock outrage, then chuckles at the thought of it.

Question concerning evolution of his stage act, his references to give himself even may by somebody obliges believes for enemies to go un occupied off which the same convey he set assaulting one Now York where. "The four events from far two songs "One of good tortoise often times marries in fail, while must at pace legislation what can't do anything at all. But you may realise the point and drink and cry, and me, I just can't care at all." But by love easy quietly asking free of overman's welters but his own. A red, strange and very likeable man.

RAY FOX-CUMMING

Lou Reed: the Sinatra of 70's

LOU REED SURE is a ...d. The day before this was supposed to [...]

his two solo albums, you can't help but recognize Lou's desperate urge to hop into Frank Sinatra's cocktail-lounge brothel-creepers, and take over as King Crooner for the Closet Romantics of the '70s.

But, y'know, I just had to laugh. Wandering into the Holiday Inn situated in East Detroit, where the Reed entourage were settled in for their concert that evening where should I discover ole' Lou but holding up the bar.

He wasn't swallowing razorblades, but was pouring equally lethal double-scotches down his golden gullet with the devil-may - care abandon of the wasted soul we all know and love.

And get that style. Those pallid, plump features, the physique of a debauched panda bear, the loose-fitting pyjamatop and baggy slacks — our boy looked like a cross between a restaurant owner and a refugee from a massage parlour.

Manager Dennis Katz helped him over to where we were seated, and drinks were ordered.

"I'm drinking two-to-one now, y'know. I've got to have the strong spirits, or else I can't taste it."

How did that affect his metabolism?

"It destroys it," muttered our hero nonchalantly.

After this tasty rejoiner, I took the bull by the horns and asked Reed how it felt to be voted second only to Keith Richard in a "Who will be the next Rock 'n' Roll casualty?" odds-on contest in a recent magazine.

"Oh really, that's fabulous. It's a real honour to be voted after Keith. Now he's a true rock 'n' roll star."

But what about the implications?

"I want to live to a ripe old age and raise water-melons," came the reply, followed through with an attempt at a piercing glare, dulled and made distant by the excesses of drink. Lou took another slug, and drawled on.

THE NEXT QUESTION concerned the young kids who come to see him these days for a deep initiation into perversion and all manner of murk.

"I don't care how they take it all. They can have it on any level they want — I've gotten past the stage of worrying if an audience is going to understand the lyrics to 'Sweet Jane' or 'Heroin'.

"The only thing that affects me about 'Heroin' is actually performing that song on stage. I go through it all again. I get pretty involved.

"Sure, I can still emphasise with all those songs I wrote before. 'I'm Waiting For The Man'. Yeah, sure, I went through all that and I can still relate to it all. But old aficionados of mine are criticising my new work for all the wrong reasons. They want another 'Sweet Jane' or 'Sister Ray', and I can't give it to them."

The differences between the first and second solo albums were incredible in the general concepts and attitudes towards themes. Where had all the posi[...]on of that first record disap[...]?

[...] first album [...] [...] beach.

seemed better than calling it Omaha.'
Lou Reed

'It's involved with violence, both mental and physical. It takes place for real in Berlin in 1973. The really important thing is the relationship between the two major characters. The narrator is filling you in from his point of view, and his point of view is not particularly pleasant.' *Lou Reed*

'Lou tried to make it up to me with the *Berlin* album . . . I'm from Berlin originally, and he wrote me letters saying Berlin was me.' *Nico*

'The reactions have been very interesting. They don't seem to form a middle, there's just two extremes. One reaction is that

they're just appalled, they hate it, really hate it. Like *Rolling Stone*'s reviewer gave it a very short, succinct review in which he said that I should be physically punished. On the other hand the *New York Times* called it a colossal work of art or something, and someone called it the *Sergeant Pepper* of the seventies, which quite insults me actually. Really I didn't expect either of those reactions. It was such a strain on everybody involved in doing that thing, just physically as well as emotionally, and mentally it took a real toll.' *Lou Reed*

'It's certainly not a party album, it's not something you enjoy. Like Nico said to me, "Lou, why do you encourage suicide?" So I said, "Now Nico that's not true," and you know she couldn't understand a word of it. I don't even know what made her think it was about suicide in the first place.' *Lou Reed*

'Adults like the album, younger people do have trouble relating to it. Like suicide, or having the kids taken away, only means something to an older person – it doesn't hit a kid, but older people flee when they hear side two of *Berlin*, especially women, and especially women who are mothers. They get enormously depressed, but they like it. It's like my reaction and Bobby Ezrin's reaction. Like when we listened to it all, and Bobby turned to me and said "Lou, I think the best idea is that we put it in a box, put the box in a closet, leave it there and don't listen to it again." And I think he was right. But now it's out, and it's there, and other people have to cope with it.' *Lou Reed*

'It wasn't my idea to put actual children's voices crying on side two, for example, but look at the effect of it. People have said to me, "Oh Lou, that's too heavy-handed", but some of them have said it while crying. It's distinctly unpleasant, no matter which way you look at it.' *Lou Reed*

'You're paying your money for a bummer, is

one way of looking at it. Logic would have dictated doing something lighter and more commercial after *Transformer*, but we wanted to do this.' *Lou Reed*

'RCA definitely dictated that I don't do it again – they made me promise not to do it for at least two albums. They want more commercial records and I think I want that too, but then *Berlin* wasn't totally uncommercial. The sales are very interesting. They don't go up, but they don't go down. Just steady. If I was to die, then it would sell sure enough. I mean, since Jim Croce died he's had three albums in the top ten in America.' *Lou Reed*

'*Berlin* is bitter, uncompromising and one of the most fully realised concept albums. Prettiness has nothing to do with it, nor does good taste, good manners or good morals. Reed is one of the handful of serious artists working in popular music today, and you'd think by now people would stop

1973 was the year Lou squirmed his way up the Thirty and into the con- sness of the sheltered es on both sides of the . Sure, stran- hang...

and give him his due, Lou's made the grand connection with pure undiluted grace.

"Walk On The Wild Side" was the number, delivered by Reed with a ...ce which immediately placed ... his previous

acceptance.

Those terrible "gay" consciousness songs, the limp-wristed rockers, t̶ cover—they all added up to pr͡ Lou Reed's first real artist! albu—

preaching at him.' *Timothy Ferris, Rolling Stone*

'I do think that the album is adult, but when we do those same songs live they are much more direct with a group, and the thirteen year olds can relate to some of it.' *Lou Reed*

'People don't deserve good lyrics because they never listen to them these days. That's why the melody has to be good. When I have a lyric that I think everybody will like though, I won't drown it out. If it's a secret lyric I'll bury it. I don't print lyrics on record sleeves, except with *Berlin*, and then they wrote them with a quill pen, the stupid fuckers! They wrote them out in longhand because they thought that was chic. I could have killed them.' *Lou Reed*

The nature of the album clearly reflected the events and mood-swings in Reed's life at the time. Warhol superstar Andrea 'Whips' Feldman had recently committed suicide and, although this wasn't widely known at the time, Lou's own wife Betty tried to end her life shortly afterwards.

'During the recording sessions, my old lady – who was an asshole but I needed a female asshole to bolster me up, I needed a syco- phant who could bounce around and she fit the bill, but she called it love, ha! – she tried to commit suicide in the bathtub at the hotel. Cut her wrists – she lived. But we had to have a roadie there with her from then on.' *Lou Reed*

The recording took its toll on all concerned particularly Ezrin who, when he returned to the States from London, suffered a breakdown.

'It was a heroin rebound. I would rather have had a nervous breakdown. I didn't know what heroin was till I went to England on this gig. I suppose that's a breakdown, a chemical breakdown. We were all seriously ill. It took me a long time to get on my feet. I paid a heavy price. It put me out of commission for quite a while.' *Bob Ezrin*

'We killed ourselves psychologically on that album. We went so far into it that it was kinda hard to get out.' *Lou Reed*

'I had to do *Berlin*. If I hadn't done it I'd have gone crazy. If I hadn't got it out of my hair, I would have exploded. It was a very painful album to make. I don't want to have to go through it again, having to say those words over and over and over.' *Lou Reed*

'The way that album was overlooked, was probably the biggest disappointment I ever faced.' *Lou Reed*

'I wasn't exactly exhilarated or thrilled by the whole thing, *Lou Reed* and *Transformer*. Boredom isn't the proper word. I knew things weren't right and I was waiting. Like my marriage, it was kind of a pessimistic act – nothing else to do at the time. Then one day it dawned on me that if you don't like it you can always walk out. And as soon as that becomes clear, it was all very simple.' *Lou Reed*

Lou and Betty were divorced in Autumn 1973. The marriage had lasted less than a year.

'Everyone should have a divorce once, I can recommend it.' *Lou Reed*

'The glitter people know where I'm at, the gay people know where I'm at. I make songs up for them. I was doing that in '66 except

that people were a lot more uptight then.' *Lou Reed*

Taking the Berlin *album on the road then, Lou enjoyed a successful tour, and decided to release a recording of his New York Academy concert (from the tail end of 1973) as a live album,* Rock'n'Roll Animal. *It was released just a matter of months after* Berlin.

'Towards the end, they started rushing the stage, these guys were yelling out, "We love you Lou!" and one jumped up and says, "Give us a kiss", and these chicks, only about fourteen, were holding me . . . it was all just fun..' *Lou Reed*

'Well, the band [featuring Dick Wagner and Steve Hunter] is so really good that we just wanted to record it, to catch it at the moment in time. There's a lot of new arrangements of my songs and I also wanted

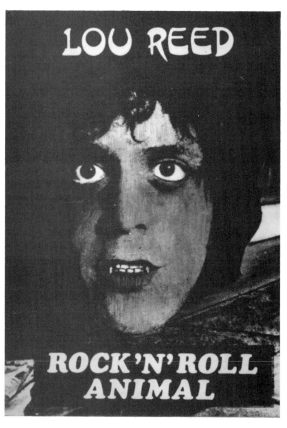

LEFT: COVER OF A MANCHESTER-BASED FANZINE ON REED, PUBLISHED IN 1978.

ROLLING STONE, MARCH 28, 1974

RECORDS

The Beauty of Decay

Rock n Roll Animal
Lou Reed

By Timothy Ferris

This is a record to be played loud. Like a Formula One car, it doesn't really begin to perform until it's pushed close to the limit. As background music it isn't much, but powered up on a strong system loud enough to make enemies a quarter-mile away, *Rock n Roll Animal*—recorded live at Lou Reed's Academy of Music concert December 21st—is, well, very fine.

Making enemies is all tied up with Lou Reed, anyway. I first heard Reed when he was part of the Velvet Underground nearly ten years ago, when somebody played "Heroin" in the Pi Kappa Alpha fraternity house at Northwestern University; it took the assembled brothers about 20 seconds to yell, "What is that shit?" and shut it off. In those days you could offend almost anybody between the Hudson River and the Sierra Nevadas just by playing a touch of Velvet Underground. If Reed's songs didn't sicken them—"Heroin," the only major pop number to praise shooting smack, or "Venus In Furs," with its loving invocation of boys kissing boots and writhing under the lash—his singing would. Smirking, arrogant, uncaring, he occupied the antarctic of rock.

What is surprising is that he should have the same effect today. One would have thought we had all grown up. When *Berlin*—the most controversial of Reed's solo albums—was released a few months ago, Reed was once again "disgusting" and "degenerate." Stephen Davis, writing in this magazine, characterized the record as "a distorted and degenerate demimonde of paranoia, schizophrenia, degradation, pill-induced violence and suicide."

Which it is. But I fail to see how that makes it a bad record. *Berlin* is bitter, uncompromising and one of the most fully realized concept albums. Prettiness has nothing to do with art, nor does good taste, good manners or good morals. Reed is one of the handful of serious artists working in popular mu-

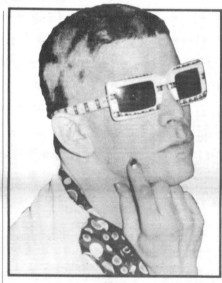

If there is redemption in Lou Reed's work beyond his honesty and musical brilliance, it is his courage.

sic before Reed takes the stage, which establishes that, unlike some of his past backup groups, this one is first-rate. The rest of the side is devoted to a towering, unsettling version of "Heroin." Each listener can personally decide the morality of this song ("Heroin, it's my wife and it's my life") as a performance it is sinister and stunning, rooted in a treacherous organ and strung tautly on a set of vaulting guitar riffs. The piece has the atmosphere of a cathedral at black mass, where heroin is God.

Side two begins with "White Light/White Heat," a tidy piece of elemental rock, and closes with "Rock 'n' Roll," a good, driving concert tune which, on the record, is entertaining but runs rather long. Between these two is "Lady Day"—like "Heroin," a great performance

the words over an organ continuo counterpointed by lead guitar riffs that come down like the clap of doom.

For some reason the musicians are not given credit on the album. They are Pentti Glen, drums; Prakash John, bass; Ray Colcord, keyboards; and most notably, Dick Wagner and Steve Hunter, guitars.

Rock n Roll Animal is much less claustrophobic and oppressive than *Berlin*, but many people will probably loathe it anyway. Faggots, junkies and sadists are not very pleasant, but theirs are the sensibilities Reed draws upon. His songs offer little hope. Nothing changes, nothing gets better. As Reed said of *Berlin*, "It's not like a TV program where all the bad things that happen to people are tolerable. Life isn't that way and neither is the

"a test of man's well-being and consciousness of power is the extent to which he can acknowledge the terrible and questionable character of things, and whether he is in any need of a faith at the end."

Which is to say by implication that there is a beauty which arises not from happiness but from wretchedness, an efflorescence of decay, as they say. Here it is. Crank the mother up.

A Singer of Sad Songs

Grievous Angel
Gram Parsons
With Emmylou Harris

describes the ... fueled Parsons ... " . . . Wild horses ... me away/Wild h... them someday. ... choose between ... gels, he broke th... welcomed both. ... Jesse Winchester ... dangerous fun. Th... results made Gram ... most convincing si... songs that I've ever h...

After leaving th... Parsons made a ... albums; *Grievous An...* pletes the cycle. Begir... the Flying Burrito ... *The Gilded Palace* ... the work progressed ... *Burrito Deluxe* and F... earlier solo effort, *GP*... quartet comprises an a... ography both faithful t... ditional musical form... themes and orginal in ... of them.

As on Parsons' earlier ... Emmylou Harris sets off G... Parsons' quavery vocals ... her cowgirl-angel voice. Th... traditional country duet... reach a zenith on two old love... songs, "Hearts On Fire" and ... "Love Hurts." The first deals ... with passion and guilt, the ... second with the anguish of ... romantic love. I find both cut ... staggeringly powerful.

Aside from a pair of pa... footstompers (Tom T. Hall'... Can't Dance" and Parsons'... Rick Grech's "Las Veg... *Grievous Angel* is Pars... most serious album. His fir... than-usual (but no less p... tive) voice, Emmylou's h... antly lovely singing, the ... tive playing of the Elvis... ley band members and a... all contribute to the r... sense of solemn pc... fulness.

On the eerie "Medle... From Northern Qu... Parsons gives a make-l... live performance befor... imaginary crowd of b... breaking country boys... recognize his tunes fro... first note. Parsons seem... saying that this is whe... might have wound up if he... followed the traditional pa... His treatment of the imagir... scenario might be interpreted... disdainful, but as he and En... mylou convincingly sing "an o... song from a long time back" (... own "Hickory Wind"), there ... suggestion of regret as well...

Parsons employed cou... conventions in his songwrit... as well as his singing, and i... often hard to separate his ori... inals from the Harlan How... and Boudleaux Bryant tu... he recorded. His best writ...

to record them like that – songs from the Velvet Underground like "Sweet Jane", "White Light", and "Rock'n'Roll", as well as straighter versions of songs from *Berlin*, though in the end we only used "Lady Day" on the album because we put on a fourteen minute version of "Heroin".' *Lou Reed*

'I like the direction my career is going right now. It has more direction and cohesiveness. I don't think that I'm a singer, with or without a guitar. I give dramatic readings, that are almost my tunes. Did you know that my real voice has never been heard. What they usually do in the studio is to speed up the vocal track and make my voice higher. I scream when I play live, because when you scream your voice goes up.' *Lou Reed*

'*Rock'n'Roll Animal* was made because we heard the tapes and liked them – I really liked them.' *Lou Reed*

'This is a record to be played loud. Like a Formula One car, it doesn't really begin to perform until it's pushed close to the limit. As background music it isn't much, but powered up on a strong system loud enough to make enemies a quarter mile away, *Rock'n'Roll Animal* is well, very fine . . . There is a beauty which arises not from happiness but from wretchedness, an efflorescence of decay, as they say. Here it is . . . crank the mother up.' *Timothy Ferris, Rolling Stone*

'*Rock'n'Roll Animal* is a clarification of my old work . . . I think. I've had my hit single and I want all those kids to know what came before that, because they don't know, and I want them to know exactly what predated "Walk On The Wild Side".' *Lou Reed*

'He looks like a monkey on a chain, court geek – listen to him scramble to a corner, damaged and grotesque, huddled in rodent terror. Animal Lou. Lashing out in a way that could easily make the current S&M

trend freeze in its shallow tracks. And the audience cheers after each song, we're with you, yeah, we always loved all those songs, ha-ha-ha. Well, he hates you.' *Chrissie Hynde, reviewing* Rock'n'Roll Animal *in NME.*

'Lou thinks that by sticking to his guns he'll succeed, and he has. He's got the whole sickness market tied up.' *John Cale*

Following the release of Rock'n'Roll Animal, *Lou appeared in public looking pale and gaunt, his hair cropped close to his skull with Maltese crosses shaved into the side. The Nazi connotations were too much for his manager Dennis Katz to take, and Reed was eventually forced to comply with good taste. What no-one forced him to do however, was get his act together – the wasted look was now less a pose than a disturbing reality.*

LOU'S METAMORPHOSIS FROM PHANTOM TO ANIMAL IS COMPLETE.

'It's fabulous being a blonde, especially when the dark roots begin to show. It's so trashy.' *Lou Reed*

By the time it came to recording his next album, Sally Can't Dance – *in Spring 1974 – Lou was scarcely capable of getting a grip on proceedings, so that much of the quality control was left to producer Steve Katz, his manager's brother. Ironically the album proved his most successful to date. Recorded at New York's Electric Lady Studios, other musicians included Danny Weiss (guitar), Prakash John (bass), Michael Fonfara (keyboards), Richard Dharma and Pentti Glan (drums).*

'They'd make a suggestion and I'd say, "Oh, alright". I'd do the vocals in one take, in twenty minutes, and then it was goodbye.' *Lou Reed*

'As an artist Lou was not totally . . . there. He had to be propped up like a baby with things done for him and around him. Clearly this was the situation he wanted.' *Steve Katz*

'It was produced in the slimiest way possible.' *Lou Reed*

'I hate *Sally Can't Dance*. I just can't write songs you can dance to. I make an effort, and *Sally Can't Dance* was an effort. But I despise that record. "Ennui" is not bad. You notice how I change my opinion of the album with the mention of that song. I like "Ennui", there's always an isolated moment on every album that I really like. It's the track that most people skip, I suspect. It must be, it's the one I like.' *Lou Reed*

'This is fantastic – the worse I am, the more it sells. If I wasn't on the record at all next time around, it would probably go number one.' *Lou Reed*

'I like these songs a lot. I think they're the best I ever did. There's no concept, but I notice as I listen to them over and over again that inter-personal theme seems to be running through.' *Lou Reed*

'I'm not in this game for the money or to be a star. It just gives me a good chance to look at lots of different kinds of people. I collect them, just certain special ones.' *Lou Reed*

The subsequent promotional tour became notorious when Lou simulated 'shooting-up' heroin on stage. During one particular performance, while the band played 'Heroin', Lou appeared to inject himself with a syringe. It's not certain whether it contained heroin, or just water.

'My songs are little plays and I give myself a big role, but they're different people. After a while maybe it should dawn on people that it all can't be the same person.' *Lou Reed*

ALWAYS ONE STEP AHEAD OF FASHION – LOU REED PEROXIDE IN PARIS IN 1974.

WANTED

LOU REED
DEAD OR ALIVE
(What's the difference)
for transforming a whole generation
of young Americans into faggot junkies.

Stevie Wonder ● Roxy & Eno ● Tina Turner's Rod ● Alex Harvey

MARCH 1975
U.K. 35P

America's Only Rock 'n' Roll Magazine

creem

BAD COMPANY
Can't Get Enough

MICK TAYLOR
Shatters
STONES

Did the
WHO
Disband?

SPACE ROCK
Extravaganza with
Nektar, Tangerine Dream,
Triumvirat, ELP, Pink Floyd,
Hawkwind, Yes, And
Mike Oldfield

BTO Bad Mouth Guess Who?

LOU REED
KING OF THE SLAG HEAP
Lester Bangs Dukes It
Out With the Rock 'n' Roll
Animal in a Vicious,
No-Holds-Barred
Interview

Exclusive Interview:
TOWNSHEND
Tooth and Nail with
Daltrey, Moon
and Entwistle

Star's Cars Poster
Genesis-Labelle
Bryan Ferry
James Bond

Creemmate of the Month

During the US dates in the autumn of 1974, Lou met and fell in love with Rachel, a transvestite, whom he immediately chose to share his life with. 'She' would prove to be a major influence on his life and work for the next four years.

'I met Rachel in a late night club in Greenwich Village. I'd been up for days as usual, and everything was at that super-real glowing stage. I walked in and there was this amazing person, this incredible head, kind of vibrating out of it all. Rachel was wearing this amazing make-up and dress, and was obviously in a different world to anyone else in the place. Eventually I spoke and she

LOU REED: "Sally Can't Dance" (RCA). In a way I hope that this is the last album that Lou Reed ever makes. There's no longer any way of ... that ... the ... und, ...cing ...dge ...dis-

... and ... with ... d of ...ssics ...eavy ... pro-..., in-...nder

...there ...cuts ...istic ...just ...his ...And ...his ...head ...erms ...l the ...hich ...ll to ...lbum ...dis-...it's ...wish ...long ...nove ...too ...skin ...leath ...come ...This ...more ...ody, ...hat ...nd ...he ...'s

LOU REED: balancing on the edge of dis-intergration

Give up, Lou!

BLONDES HAVE MORE FUN – AND TAKE MORE FLAK. LOU'S SHORT-LIVED CHANGE OF IMAGE WAS ACCOMPANIED BY A RISING CRESCENDO OF MEDIA CRITICISM.

came home with me. I rapped for hours and hours while Rachel just sat there looking at me, saying nothing. At the time I was living with a girl, a crazy blonde lady, and I kind of wanted us all three to live together, but somehow it was too heavy for her. Rachel just stayed on and the girl moved out. Rachel was completely disinterested in who I was and what I did. Nothing could impress her. He'd hardly heard my music, and didn't like it all that much when he did.' *Lou Reed*

L'HOMME EN NOIR

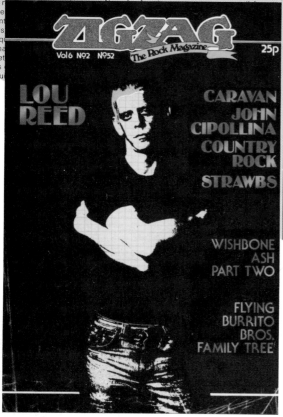

ABOVE: REED'S POPULARITY IN FRANCE HAS ALWAYS REMAINED HIGH. RIGHT: SOUVENIR PROGRAMME FOR THE EXTENSIVE TOURING OF 1974.

During the early months of 1975, Lou began to worry friends and colleagues with the state of his health. Looking increasingly weaker, and seemingly more drug-dependent than ever, the 'Phantom Of Rock' (as his record company had tagged him during the Transformer *period) seemed to be teetering close to the brink. A European tour had to be abandoned following a reported 'nervous collapse', while weeks later a festival trek was scrapped in New Zealand due to his poor physical state. The problem would later emerge as a temporary breakdown in his relationship with his transvestite partner, Rachel.*

'Reed had a personal problem of such magnitude that he was unable to perform.'
Wellington Evening Post

Lou Reed

A THEATREGRAPHICS PUBLICATION

LOU REED ("Goodnight Ladies" at London Rainbow)

photo: MICK ROCK

walkerprints

...and there's even some EVIL MOTHERS they're gonna tell you EVERYTHING is just DIRT

LOU REED
a fallen knight

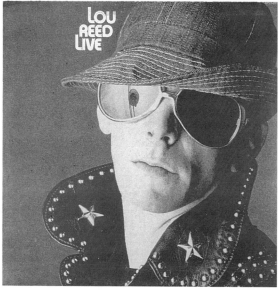

LOU REED LIVE

'Reed had a very very personal problem that should never have damn well happened. It's so personal and serious that I can't even tell you about it off the record. If you can imagine what it's like to get a call from the other side of the world, and be told that your mother was not only a drug addict but a hooker, and that she'd hooked some of your friends, then you might be able to understand how he was feeling.' *Ron Blackmore, promoter*

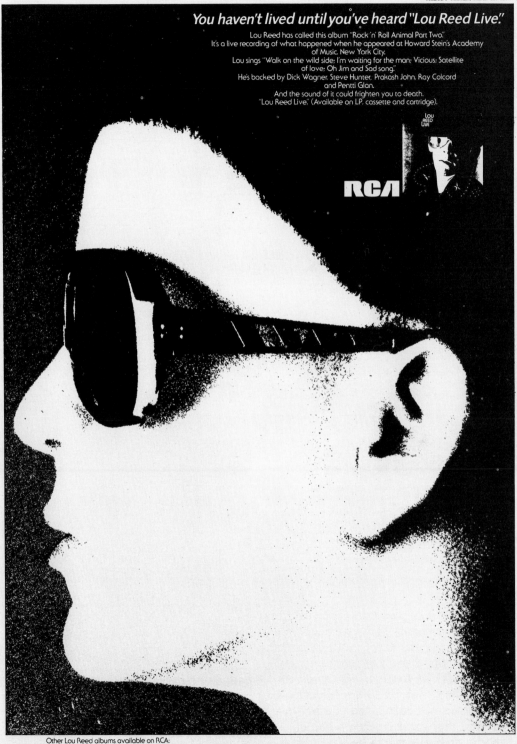

You haven't lived until you've heard "Lou Reed Live."

Lou Reed has called this album "Rock 'n' Roll Animal Part Two."
It's a live recording of what happened when he appeared at Howard Stein's Academy
of Music, New York City.
Lou sings "Walk on the wild side; I'm waiting for the man; Vicious; Satellite
of love; Oh Jim and Sad song."
He's backed by Dick Wagner, Steve Hunter, Prakash John, Ray Colcord
and Pentti Glan.
And the sound of it could frighten you to death.
"Lou Reed Live." (Available on LP, cassette and cartridge).

RCA

BRANDO ·· RAMONES ·· GIRLS ·· LEGS

PUNK

NUMBER 1 JAN.

50¢

HOLMSTROM

LOU REED

LEFT: COVER OF THE RARE AND CLASSIC US FANZINE
***PUNK* ISSUE NUMBER 1. BELOW: RCA WASTES MONEY**
ADVERTISING *METAL MACHINE MUSIC*.

In July 1975 Lou released his first double album, the notorious Metal Machine Music, *which had been recorded in the star's home studio. Produced by Reed, the work featured no other musicians. On release, the four sides of almost sheer noise were greeted with ridicule and bemusement from most reviewers, the exception being Lester Bangs who described the feedback package as 'the greatest album of all time'.*

'It was a giant "Fuck You". I put out *Metal Machine Music* to clear the air and get rid of all those fucking assholes who show up at the show and yell "Vicious" and "Walk On The Wild Side".' *Lou Reed*

'Recommended cuts: None.' *Review in* Billboard, *the US trade magazine*

'Just listen to the melody lines. There's not much that I can say about it. You see the one thing is, that no matter what else they do say about it, they can't miss the fact that it's so precise.' *Lou Reed*

'I made this for myself. I love it. This is for a certain kind of people. There aren't many.' *Lou Reed*

'I find it very relaxing. If I'm uptight, or if certain friends of mine are uptight, it relaxes them. Other people say, "Take it off" or "I'm leaving". So it's a good way of clearing a room. It's not done as a joke.' *Lou Reed*

'I suggest that "serious listeners" spend their money on something else. It's not meant for them.' *Lou Reed*

Although the timing of the album's release seemed to suit Reed's aims perfectly, the fact is that he had been playing with the idea of such a record for quite some time, right back to the early days with the Velvets, after he had come across the work of LaMonte Young.

'I've got something here that I mean by heavy metal. I had to wait a couple of years

there, running all through it, little pastoral parts, but they go by like – bap! in five seconds. Beethoven's Fifth, or Mozart . . . The Glass Harp . . . Eroica. I used pretty obvious ones. But there's about seventeen more going at the same time. It just depends which one you catch.' *Lou Reed*

'I've been thinking about doing it ever since I've been listening to LaMonte Young. I had also been listening to Xenakis a lot.' *Lou Reed*

'No-one I know has listened to it all the way through, including myself.' *Lou Reed*

'I suggest people don't buy it before they know what it sounds like.' *Lou Reed*

'I'm gonna get killed for this . . . RCA is in a panic. They don't know how to copyright it. How do you take musical notation on it? I said, "Look, don't worry. Nobody's gonna cover it." I can't see The Carpenters doing their version of it.' *Lou Reed*

'We just let it wash through the system in a low-key way.' *RCA Spokesman*

'I care about the people who bought it, thinking it was my latest rock release. A lot of people may feel ripped off and I understand and apologise for this.' *Lou Reed*

'In this, the best of all possible worlds, I would like to say that *Metal Machine Music* was ill-timed and misrepresented and I apologise and hope that my new album, *Coney Island Baby*, can make up for any difficulties and disappointments that *Metal Machine Music* has caused.' *A Lou Reed 'statement' courtesy of RCA Records*

'I didn't apologise for it. If you read the apology – well, I don't talk the way the apology was written. The apology the record company put out was meant for rock dealers.' *Lou Reed*

so I could get the equipment, now I've got it and it's done. I could have sold it as electronic classical music, except that it's heavy metal, no kidding around.' *Lou Reed*

Lou even claimed, at one stage, that Metal Machine Music *had originally been offered to the head of his label's classical division.*

'He loved it. He said we really must put it out. I said no way, because it seems hypocritical, like saying the really smart complicated stuff is over here in the classical bin – while the shit rock'n'roll goes over there where the schmucks are.' *Lou Reed*

'There's all kinds of symphonic rip-offs in

THE=only 40¢=NUMBER 41

BACKDOOR MAN

R HARDCORE ROCK'N'ROLLERS ONLY!

OU REED'S NEW ALBUM—NOISE A GO GO

ROLLING STONES on tour

NEW ORDER still talking ABOUT IGGY, BOWIE, J. SINCLAIR

the Punk goes girl crazy!

Teen Dreaming with the Tubes

concert & record reviews Aerosmith John Cale Janis Joplin Nico ZZ Top

South Bay Bands

THE FANZINE *BACKDOOR MAN* REVIEWS *METAL MACHINE MUSIC* – ONE OF THE VERY FEW MAGAZINES TO BOTHER TO DO SO.

'It was all so *boring*. Then along came *Metal Machine Music*. It was like a bomb. The idea was good in itself, but for the full impact you had to go through all the motions of execution.' *Lou Reed*

At odds again with his manager Dennis Katz over demos for his next studio album, it's possible that Lou was trying to rid himself of a man he saw as an unsuitable representative. Planned or otherwise, Katz couldn't cope with Reed's apparent disrespect for commerciality, and quit soon after the release of Metal Machine Music. *Lou replaced him with booking agent Johnny Podell.*

'There were rumours that I couldn't stand tours because I was on dope and my mind was going. I put out *Metal Machine Music* precisely to put a stop to all of it. It wasn't ill-advised at all. It did what it was supposed to do.' *Lou Reed*

'There is a lot of impressive disinformation on the back of the cover, very, very pretty, one hour and six minutes of feedback noise. It has some distractive convoluted ramblings inside the cover, but it's a trap and I'll avoid it if I can. Electronics is boring anyway, it should be left to the professionals, no sniffers please.' *John Cale on* Metal Machine Music

'I just want everyone to know that the next album isn't going to be son of *Metal Machine*. I think I shoulda charged like $78.99 for *Metal Machine* so people stop bitching that they were ripped off. They oughta be happy that it was even released. Even if it wasn't released for that long.' *Lou Reed*

'It's more complicated than the average reviewer can understand . . . especially for cretins. Anyone can review "Louie Louie".' *Lou Reed*

'This to me is what rock journalists do, they rip-off, make fun of musicians . . . y'know, and sell to morons. Written by morons for morons.' *Lou Reed*

'Show me a journalist who isn't a whore, and I'll show you a man.' *Lou Reed*

Lou did have time for one critic however, Lester Bangs, with whom he developed a famed love/hate relationship over the years – until the latter's drug-assisted death in April 1982.

'The best way to get anything publicised is to tell Lester. "Please don't print that," and he'll print it. The very best way is to let him overhear something accidentally on purpose.' *Lou Reed*

5. Taking No Prisoner: 1975-1978

EVEN AT the time that Metal Machine Music *was being released in 1975, Lou was writing, rehearsing and even performing with John Cale at St Marks Church, New York, new material which would form the backbone for his subsequent* Coney Island Baby *album – a collection of songs clearly inspired by his relationship with Rachel. Lou was joined in New York's Media Sound Studios by Bob Kulick (guitar), Bruce Yaw (bass), Michael Suchorsky (drums) and co-producer Godfrey Diamond.*

'I didn't sleep through this one, I could play *Coney Island Baby* to people and be really proud of it.' *Lou Reed*

'No more bullshit, dyed hair faggot junkie trip – the worse I was, the more they bought. It was incredible. *Sally Can't Dance* went top ten – and it sucks!' *Lou Reed*

'I mimic me probably better than anybody. So if everybody else is making money ripping me off, I figured maybe I'd better get in on it. I created Lou Reed, I have nothing even faintly in common with that guy, but I can play him well. Really well.' *Lou Reed*

'I would have left it with *Metal Machine* and the Velvets. Everyone connected with *Coney Island Baby* knows that to have me record it, *Coney Island Baby* couldn't be tampered with, there's no outside disruptive forces, no advice, no looking over my shoulder. It's how I used to feel when the Velvets were together, but it's not a nostalgic trip. 'Cos the old Velvets stuff was about ten years ahead, so if I start doing my part now, I should be right in tune with 1979.' *Lou Reed*

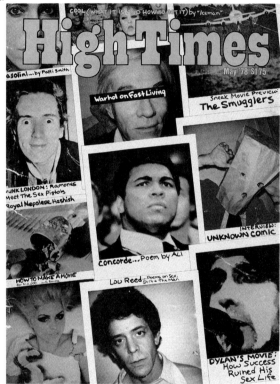

THE ALTERNATIVE HIPPY MAGAZINE *HIGH TIMES* FEATURES SOME OF LOU REED'S POETRY IN 1978.

Dennis Katz, Lou's former manager, made several attempts to prevent the album even being recorded, delivering law suits which made bold claims on the musician's right to work. Details have never really emerged, but it's widely recognised that Lou's lack of interest in business dealings had inevitably led to him signing inappropriate contracts.

'I made *Coney Island Baby* and was served three times with three separate subpoenas. One before, one during and one after.' *Lou Reed*

HOW TO SUCCEED IN TORTURE WITHOUT REALLY TRYING

OR.

Louie Come Home, All is Forgiven

BY LESTER BANGS

"Ugh. Well all right, but why cancha just get physical like a human?" — William Burroughs, *Naked Lunch*

This is not Round Three.

By now I am sure there are many you out there who may have gro bit weary of this Lou Reed subje tell the truth, I'm almost getti with Lou myself, and he is ce my hero anymore. My new President Amin of Uganda.

You may, however, wonde such ar could b record compar of Ame

In ca Metal l thing in pany, l we hav record ing but corded back ag split do separat shrieks audien possibl sentien sible no playing ions: n freaks, amine numbe chemic peopl alrea it s cat of t Mu bou w

Rock New3

INTERVIEW EXCLUSIVE

LOU REED

KIM FOWLEY

WHO

SPECIAL L.A.

interview: James WILLIAMSON

'*Coney Island Baby* is me from top to bottom, and if you don't like it, stuff it . . . It has to be accessible. If you want to make records for a cult of three, OK, knock yourself out, but don't do it under an illusion. I thought *Metal Machine Music* really demonstrated that.' *Lou Reed*

'If you don't have a sense of humour with

these things, you're doomed. Andy said the hardest thing in life was to learn to say "So what". The building just fell on my leg and they had to amputate, and they took off my arm too, but so what.' *Lou Reed*

'Roadies got an expression – any time a truck blows up or an underpass clearance is ten feet and the truck is fourteen feet, and he's just taken twelve reds, and they go into it WHAM! – that's rock'n'roll.' *Lou Reed*

'It took me two weeks to write all the material, do the recording and the final mixing for *Coney Island Baby*. Look I can answer these questions in any way you want me to. If you want to believe another answer, fine, but it was two weeks.' *Lou Reed*

'On *Coney Island Baby* there's a song that goes, "I'm just a gift to the women of this world", I love that song , it's so funny. One

83

is supposed to improve with age like good wine, I'm sure I do.' *Lou Reed*

'Anything can be sex, getting off is sex,

getting to an audience is sex, looking is sex. Your body is a framework with infinite possibilities, it's just a question of tapping one of them.' *Lou Reed*

Lou was at the height of his relationship with Rachel at the end of 1975.

'I enjoy being around Rachel, that's all there is to it. Whatever it is I need, Rachel seems to supply it, at the least we're equal.' *Lou Reed*

He was also actively engaged in writing some poetry for publication, as well as producing an album (Wild Angel) *for his friend Nelson Slater – who seemed to arrive out of nowhere, only to return there very quickly. This would mark Lou's*

How Lou Saw the White Light

An interview with Lou Reed, Godfather of punk rock, by Caroline Coon in America

has kept in touch with his roots. But his claim to fame is based on something far more substantial than image credibility alone.

He has released albums like "Sally Can't Dance" which are unsuccessful when judged by the high standards he set himself, but he has never lost sight of rock 'n' roll's essential force. He has constantly reminded us what the bed-rock of the idiom is. His guitar and vocal style has had as much influence on Seventies rock as Chuck Berry's had on the Sixties.

His musical integrity has endeared him to a new generation of fans who are unable to relate to the more grandiose and sometimes pretentious endeavours of other superstars — with Lou burning the torch for raw, fundamental forms, it doesn't matter how far into middle-of-the-road reaches rock is taken by Queen, 10cc, Yes, Rod Stewart and Peter Frampton. And, his new album "Rock 'n' Roll Heart" (Arista) reveals that if he is still the Prince of Decadence, then he is the spirit of rock 'n' roll's Guardian Angel as well!

Not that Lou is a completely new man. For all his speedy fitness, he is still painfully self-conscious in front of strangers. He feels he is being watched and judged moment by moment, and therefore he nervously calculates every move he makes — however slight.

After the first dinner we all had together, we went on to The Roxy to hear a favourite local combo called Stuff. Lou is caught in a dilemma — one he usually avoids since he is rarely seen in public. He is flicking his shades on and off. If he wears them he is instantly recognised yet protected behind their opaque lenses. If he twists them in his hands he is more likely to melt anonymously into the crowd. But then he feels vulnerably exposed. Meanwhile the flash bulbs pop around him.

Sitting close to Rachel, Lou looks unhappy. The rest of his band sitting at our table are clapping enthusiastically as the musicians on stage, joined for two numbers by Joe Cocker, play through a set of funky, improvised jazz. "What boring sh--!" Lou whispers to Rachel. Five minutes later we leave.

It is a typical Lou Reed contradiction to find him at the Santa Monica Civic the next night, playing the style of music he had so resoundingly condemned at the Roxy. He is having an inspirational affair with Ornette Coleman and, with Coleman's trumpet player Don Cherry joining the band for the whole Santa Monica set, Lou is deep into a new on-stage personna. He is no longer a barely coherent, introverted human piece flotsam. He is playing the role of a spirited jazz extrovert taking a night off from The New York Jazz Ensemble.

Lou and Rachel . . . happy together

It's a fine performance, if not the classic rock 'n' roll music the majority of the audience, including me, want to hear. But, his conviction and superb presentation (the band is set-up in front of 48 flickering video TV screens) pulls him through.

He performs twenty-one numbers in a two-and-a-half hour set, including "Lisa Says," "Waiting For The Man," "Walk On The Wild Side," all but four of the tracks from "Rock 'n' Roll Heart" and "White Light" as the encore.

Saying not a word between songs, he sings tenderly when he is alone in the spotlight, he is cynical, dead-pan and violent when, in "Temporary Thing," he slaps the mike as if it were someone's face. He walks across the stage like Bowie, he dances jerkily like Leo Sayer and yet, free of gimmicks and just relying on emotions, he has never been more himself. Especially when, strapping on his guitar, he tucks it up higher under his arm than any other musician.

And what a guitar! "It's an ANIMAL," breathes Lou in his hotel bedroom before the show. Indeed. A rare (fewer than fifty exist), compact, solid, unpainted hard-wood Smith-Spector, it looks more as if if it was born than carved by human hand.

Lou is holding it gently across his knees, restringing it with heavy gauge strings and polishing it with loving care. He is listening to the live tape recordings he has made of the tour so far and he seems so happy that trying to drag him away for an interview could have been a problem. But Rachel, although sick with an infected lung, is hungry. So half-an-hour later, in the maroon, nouveau-baroque extravaganza of the Beverly Wiltshire Hotel, we are having a Thanksgiving lunch.

Sipping a huge Silver Cadillac cocktail Lou worries about Rachel's health. Asking me to do a forehead-test he says "Is it hot?" Then he turns to Rachel. "How is it that I'm the voice of reason,"

reso[...]
It w[...]
be eating [...]
most ritzy [...]
little else is [...]
Thanksgiving [...]
he purposefully cult[...]
model, anti-star life style? [...]
begin. "Oh no," says Lou in his hypnotically laconic drawl.

"I didn't want to stay at the Hyatt House — the powers that be had their way — but I live quite simply in New York, on the Upper East Side in a two-roomed apartment. I don't go out much. I went through all that a long time ago. I knew all THOSE people.

"I guess it's something to do if you've never done it. But now I'd rather sit at home and play with my machine. Or I may go out and check over another guitar player or . . . well, there's only one or two people I see in New York. There's almost nobody left really.

"I'm not at all the Beverly Wiltshire type. But there was a time when people didn't see it that way. If I was around the 'scene' there was a reason for it. I needed certain people. A friend of mine said to me once, and it really seemed to be true, that I'm an actor who brings out the idiocy in people. And I do it by doing nothing. And it's so funny.

"Like the way people interpret my lyrics. Rock 'n' roll's not supposed to have lyrics printed on the back but there are fanatics who believe my lyrics word for word — things which are just impossible. I still don't know the lyrics to "Rock 'n' Roll Heart." I make them up as I go along!"

He doesn't give the impression of being rich. Has he made any money in his career? "I made a lot of money. But I never saw it! There are law suits over that. If I had more money I'd have more toys. There's all kinds of video equipment I could have to play with. And more cassette recorders. Because I don't have enough money, I always seem to be just a step behind the latest invention."

He had quite an affluent childhood, didn't he? "I didn't starve. I know what it's like to have money. So what! My parents were self-made millionaires. On paper they were very rich. They would love me to take over the companies."

What kind of business was it? "Despicable! It has to do with numbers. If United States Steel is your client you can save them millions. Accountancy? No, a little more complicated. Tax law."

He doesn't like his parents too much then? "It's not that I don't like them. It's just that I think for all concerned it's better if we stay far apart. I have very little contact with them and the few times I have seen them just confirms the fact that we're better apart."

Would he like his career to have been any different? "That's hypothetical. Too hypothetical to consider or answer. Like — if Eisenhower had been defeated . . ."

Yes, but if his crucial album, the one he considered to be his "tour de force", had been a success, his career might have turned out very differently. "Oh 'Berlin' will see it's place in the sun some day. It's better than all the albums. And there are people who, in retrospect, are looking over their shoulders and saying 'OH! WAIT A MINUTE . . .'"

There was a musical direction in which he could have continued after "Berlin" but, because of the critical reaction, instead of developing the complex themes and fully orchestrated arrangements, he cut himself right back to basics again.

"Yes. I stopped. Why? I wasn't going to put myself through THAT again. For THAT! See, for X person, the 'Berlin' sales were very good. I was coming off 'Transformer' and I'd had a hit single. But, so that I wouldn't be bored, I wanted to see whether I could have a hit single with a BAND rather than me on my own.

"So there was this big fight with RCA. I talked them into the veracity of the whole thing, of how astute it would be to follow up "Walk On The Wild Side" with not just another hit single but with a magnificent whatever . . . So, you know, I shoved it through.

"And the record sales, compared to "Transformer," were a disaster for a normal person who was great, but for me it was a total disaster. The record company did a quick scurry around like little bunnies. But I went somnambulent. It wasn't brain rot like some people think. I just kinda did no more."

Did he expect the negative reaction? "No. But who cares about critics? 'Berlin' was an album for adults. I want to make real albums. That whole thing started because I wanted to write real songs about something that was relevant.

"I'd mastered the art of negative punk and all that with Andy (Warhol) and The Underground and that stuff is so cute. I know that whole thing. And what would have been the point in trying to be more commercial?"

Money? "Oh, you can always get THAT. But you couldn't always do a 'Berlin'. I mean, we really killed ourselves on that. Psychologically. We went so far into it that it was kinda hard to get out. Bob Ezrin (the producer) is as bad as I am. He insists on doing things the hard way.

"All you have to do is look at what I have done to know that I don't want to make money. That's so obvious. At any one of a number of points I could have gone SNAP. And instead, I purposefully f—— it up one way or another. You don't have to be bright to see that.

"At the time I just got torn to shreds. Just killed, you know. But I think the kids understood. When they look back and check it over they say 'hey, there's a very straight line!' And when they hear 'Rock 'n' Roll Heart' they say 'hey, wait a minute. What is this we're hearing.' It's been one whole line. I mean, at the peak of it, putting out 'Metal Machine Music!' I mean, nobody could miss that.

"No matter what you say about me, that was commercial suicide. It was calculated — on purpose with no 'if's' and 'but's.' The critics tried to rationalise it by saying I was afraid of stardom. Ha! Yeh? Ok. Take it any way you want. But you can't miss the fact that my very first double-album was reviewed in Billboard like — Recommended cuts: NONE.

"There's only one kind of person that would do such a thing . . . I mean, who would do such a thing. I made that double-album because that's what I wanted to do and that's what it was. And I happen to like the record, so there! And I like 'Coney Island Baby' and 'Rock 'n' Roll Heart,' so there. THERE!"

He does, it seems, react quite strongly to what critics say. "No. I didn't react. I stopped. The people around me reacted and it got out of control. And it stayed out of control. They (RCA) put out

'Rock And Roll Animal' and it was a walking time-warp to me.

"'Rock 'n' Roll Animal' has a perfect sound though. Because I mixed it. The engineer just left. He didn't know how to record it. I couldn't stand what they were doing — cleaning it up. And I went 'oh, no!' And there was another big fight. But you notice from that point on, my singing is off key and it's all a monotone bla bla bla bla. 'Rock 'n' Roll Heart' is not. It's in tune — perfect. Funny.

"When 'Metal Machine Music' was here everybody kept saying 'when are you going to do a guitar solo.' And I thought, 'after taking this load of s——, wait a minute. Hang in there.' I did do some nice stuff. Once in a while. By mistake usually."

"Sally Can't Dance" seemed to be his lowest musical ebb. "Oh, I slept through 'Sally Can't Dance' — that's no big secret. They'd make a suggestion and I'd say 'oh, all right.' I'd do the vocals in one take, in twenty minutes, and then it was 'good-bye.'

"But the worse the albums were, the more they apparently sold. And I kept thinking that somehow it would stop. But it didn't. So I decided to put a stop to it. For those who wanted to hear the real thing, and wanted to hear a guitar solo, they got 'Metal Machine Music.' And that put A STOP to it! There wasn't going to be any more records after that."

Then why, if 'Metal Machine Music' was such a calculated move, did he issue a public statement apologising for the album? "I DIDN'T apologise for it! If you read the apology — well, I don't talk the way the apology was written. The apology the record company put out was meant for rack dealers.

"As far as the rest of the people went, what I said was 'You're f—— lucky that the record came out and I should have charged 78 dollars for it! If people think it's a rip off — f—— 'em, they should be glad they got it because they're not going to get anything else.'

"That wasn't an apology! The only apology I made was that I wished RCA had done what I asked and they said they would, but of course they didn't — which was to let people hear the album before they bought it."

He has, at one time or another, disowned most of what he's ever recorded — even 'Walk On The Wild Side." Does he still feel like that about his work? "No," he replies after a very long pause. "I didn't like what 'Walk On The Wild Side' did. Or the way it was used. I was disgusted. I don't disown everything that I've done. But everything can be better."

How has he managed to keep his sense of musical identity and self-worth when, over the years, he's been under such consistant critical fire? "People say this and people say that, but if I listen to something by myself I can make up my own mind. I'm OK if I'm left alone for a while.

"I read reviews because I'm curious to see what the critics say. One will say one thing and another will say something else. But if you go by the kids you're more likely to know. It's their reaction I'm interested in."

Would he have liked to have been more commercially successful? "That's hypothetical. If I hadn't quit the Velvet Underground I'd be loaded — loaded! If I hadn't quit the group when I did we would have broken. We'd have made it. If I'd followed 'Walk On The Wild Side' with another hit, I'd have made it. But I made a point of not.

"Why? Because it wasn't the right time, it wasn't the right place, it wasn't the right people, it wasn't the right situation. I didn't want to be locked in. My background was showing!"

His penultimate album "Coney Island Baby" did seem a considered effort to be more commercial, though. Was it? "It was my last attempt with RCA. They said, you can do anything you want so long as it's not 'Metal Machine Music.'

"So I made a very stark, very bare album, very quickly. And then I watched what they did with it. And I said that's it! Now there isn't any more. From now on there's only 'Metal Machine Music.'

"The thing is," continues Lou, who has eaten only an hors d'oeuvre, eschewing a main course in favour of another large Silver Cadillac, "I couldn't go through with making another 'Metal Machine Music.' It took six years to do, from conception to initial prototype tapes to being able to afford the machinery to complete it!"

What with leaving one record label, moving to Arista and being plagued by various law suits, Lou has maintained a very low profile since 1974. Why, almost overnight, did he decide to tour again?

"I didn't tour for two years because there was no reason to. No reason to put

he [...]
char[...]
abo[...]
PLA[...]
"I [...]
Pay' [...]
that' [...]
solo, [...]
rare [...]
"It's [...]
part. [...]
live bu[...]
studio. It [...]
way it goes [...]
a sound wave. [...]
right back to the stu[...]
Velvets!"

All the while Lou is [...] and not eating, Rac[...] eaten a huge plate of [...] giving turkey, left th[...] several times to che[...] all is well at the [...] organised the car to ta[...] to the gig, worried [...] Lou's two travelling [...] ions — his miniatur[...] shunds, The Count a[...] Duke — are behaving [...] selves in the hotel [...] (they're not. They ea[...] new tape recorder [...] phones), and made [...] calls to New York —a[...] fact, the perfect aide-d[...]

Lou, occasionally co[...] to see whether eve[...] external to the inter[...] running smoothly, has [...] relaxed. Although [...] flicker of a smile b[...] his permanently grave [...] is in a buoyant fra[...] mind.

He comes across to [...] someone who, even th[...] is experiencing a cha[...] fortune, is still hiding [...] the "front" he ha[...] used when life wa[...] disasterously traumatic [...] I asked him why he [...] smiles, he replies [...] does, "inwardly" [...] typical Reedism.

All his life Lou has [...] lyrics which reveal [...] closer to his own onl[...] the words are interpr[...] meaning almost totally [...] posite to what they [...] say. For instance, on[...] porary Thing," one [...] finest tracks on "R[...] Roll Heart," Lou insi[...] a relationship he is h[...] just that — a te[...] thing.

But surely he is [...] the truth, avoiding a[...] how seriously commi[...] is to those he loves? [...] replies Lou without [...] tion. "The lady doth [...] too much! He (and [...] talks about himself [...] third person) knows [...] a temporary thing. [...] can figure that out [...] in 'Walk On The W[...] when I say 'she's de[...] know? Candy by th[...] she's dead.' But it'[...] like 'I miss you Can[...] feeling like, you know[...]

"When I heard the [...] 'Temporary Thing' I [...] 'oh, no Lou, you're [...] the edge.' You kn[...] I REALLY PLAY [...] KEEPS.' I wanted [...] know that, I wanted [...] care. Not that they [...] care. Why get that s[...]

He pauses for a[...] Then he continues: [...] reviewer wrote ab[...] 'quavering voice' on [...] Island Baby" when I'[...] ing this out to [...] Rachel.' Quavering v[...] I'd like to have him [...] minutes — just five [...] alone with him. I [...] him, you know. But y[...] really be bothered [...] kind of stuff."

Lou has always [...] emotions, his heart [...] sleeve! "They're 'H[...] I'm not being glib [...] use the third per[...] true, but the que[...] whether I'm ac[...] not. There's a lot of [...] characters running [...] all of this and I co[...] all of them. And y[...] not be anybody else [...] like to say that I w[...] and give myself the [...] part in them."

Many of his so[...] titles like "Lisa [...] "Cindy Says," [...]

I'd mastered the art of negative punk with Warhol, and that stuff is so cute

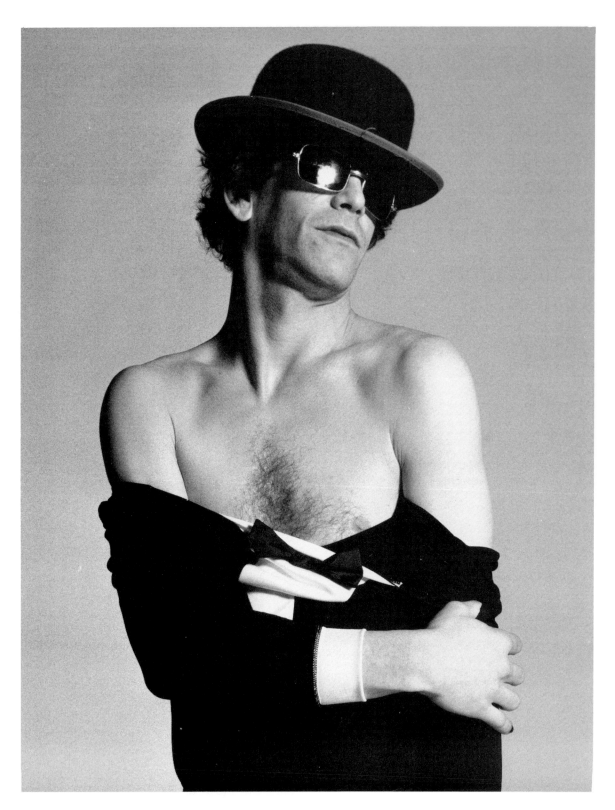

HATS OFF TO LOU REED FOR CONEY ISLAND BABY

RS 1035

No candy floss on this album just pure Lou Reed

RCA Records and Tapes

New Single **Charley's Girl** RCA 2666

last involvement with RCA. In the summer of 1976 he signed to Clive Davis's Arista label and went into the studio to record Rock And Roll Heart. Musicians included Michael Fonfara on keyboards, Bruce Yaw on bass, Michael Suchorsky on drums and Marty Fogel on sax.

FOR CONEY ISLAND BABY LOU ADOPTED A DELIBERATELY PERVERSE IMAGE.

How many times does a snake crawl out of his skin?

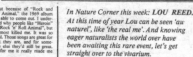

*In Nature Corner this week: **LOU REED**. At this time of year Lou can be seen 'au naturel', like 'the real me'. And knowing eager naturalists the world over have been awaiting this rare event, let's get straight over to the vivarium.*

But because of "Rock and Roll Animal," the 1969 album was able to come out. I understand why people like "Heroin" on "Rock 'n' Roll Animal", but it almost killed me. It was so awful. Those songs are great for that they are, and for somebody else they'd still be great, for me it really made me

But I kept going through it because it did what it supposed to. It got the '69 out. It got MGM to release all those Velvet things. They've repackaged it 700 ways, and we still any royalties, but that point.

always arranged it so as could come out . . . the live set, now that's an album I really love. If you want to know what Max's was really like — and now you can't — but there, for real because Brigid was just sitting with her little Sony re-. It's in mono, you can't but you can hear just We're out of tune, per it's Sunday night, regulars are there, arroll's trying to get and they're talking about war . . . we were the band. There it is.

The main thing was to get the Velvet's stuff out. Then I could be in a position to do an album that was me, all the way through.

What about Berlin?

was great what Bobby (Ezdid. If I was in charge, I'd've done it somewhat differtly. But he did a great job. on that album

you try to get a copy. You can't get 'em, you can't order them, they're in bins someplace. I have orders in five stores. They've disappeared off the face of the earth. Nico doing "The End" is so unbelievable — and John . . . but then you listen to "Slow Dazzle". The thing is he's trying to get the Velvet's thing too. We talk about it all the time.

Do you think the re-packages have served the Velvets well?

Well, they leave out a lot of the heavy stuff. It's always

"Sister Ray", it's always "Heroin" . . . and I'm really glad they're on it — you can hear what we were doing 11 years ago. That's why we closed the "Coney Island Baby" sessions. No producers, nobody to say. When we did "Sister Ray", we turned up to ten flat out. leakage all over the place. That's it. They asked us what we were going to do. We said we're going to start. They said who's playing bass? We said there is no bass. They asked us

when it ends. We didn't know. When it ends. that's when it ends.

What about the other members of the group?

Maureen (Tucker, drums) was perfect on that song. She works for IBM now, and you can tell from us that she was born to the job. All we wanted was someone who could play on a telephone book. Sterling (Morrison, guitarist) is teaching English some place, wishing he was in a rock and roll band. When he was in a rock and roll band, he wanted to be in school.

Like the Velvets were the best kept secret in the world, but they didn't go without having their effect. The records that come out now say 'Lou Reed and the Velvet Underground', but to me that's depressing. It wasn't me alone; if John had gotten popular ahead of me, then it would have been John Cale and the Velvet Underground.

The thing was just to get those albums out. I couldn't, or John couldn't leave them just sitting there. So I went and decided to get popular. It's as simple as that. And John's doing the same thing. Eventually he'll

put out the album he really out. I used to plead with him put out some of the things came up with — he had record oh, Christ! It was great. An thing he does is great. In a book, people ought to be he's even on a record.

The thing is he was right a to record them and put them his albums, because if he did would just be the Velvets over again. The track you tie Because they don't want to he that. You have to get popu first. I got to the point where put 'Metal Machine Mu out. That was like, okay, n let's stop messing around.

At the very least . . .

First of all, I happen to lo that album. I don't care wh anybody says. It's fun . . .

When did you first sta thinking about it?

Oh . . . maybe as far back when John used to work w Lamonte Young (avant-ga composer of the drone-t "Dream Symphonies"). It w a long, long time. It's way mo complex than people realise, t that's all right. I wasn't going put it out even; I made it myself. John and I were alwa making tapes. A lot are still c culating around. We may d soundtracks for undergrou movies of the time . . . we ways encouraged bringing ta recorders to our jobs.

What did RCA think abo "Metal Machine"?

Well, at first they were go to put it on Red Seal, the cla sical music label. The hea classical music heard it, and know who I'd been listening But it got put out on the p label because it was a Lou Re record, and it was a real Lo Reed record. No bullshitting ound. You want heavy met You got off on "Rock 'n' R Animal"? Okay, shmuck, n we'll give some heavy metal.

The thing is that it's a r trip. Not for most people t cause they get scared off, an set it up that way. There a frequencies in there that are s against FCC law to use, th use them in surgery. B if you put certain combinations tones togeth and kee building on th harmonically there's 7,0 melodies. Like Sibel will go sliding by, whos It's all really speed, to say least. I don't say that facetio ly. The thing is that ther enough there to have fun with wasn't going to put an instru tional pamphlet in with These who knew would kno and those who didn't, scr 'em.

Were you pleased at reception?

The rock reviews tore the w out of it. Not that's to be expe ed. Which is exactly why Je and I didn't put out a wh slew of things. Look at w you're dealing with. Look at co's stuff that's out. With t and 50 cents you can get on subway. I never put out double-album before. I control of that thing graphics on dow gave them a fin already mastere too . . . in quad!

People don' 16 minutes an on each side; I was trying squ'ely sav entrop if

'Lou and I were friends during this period when he was dissatisfied with his existing label. He called me and said, "I see where you're going with Arista, I see what you're doing. Would you be interested in signing me?" The lawyers got together and we worked out a deal . . .I'll never forget that Lou took me on a tour of Manhattan, the likes of which I've never had. It was an amazing experience. Seeing Lou Reed's world was a very revealing, very eye opening situation.' *Clive Davis*

'There was just Rachel and me living at the Gramercy Park Hotel on $15 a day, while the lawyers were trying to figure out what to do with me. Then I got a call from Clive Davis. I felt like saying, "You mean you want to be seen with me in public?" I knew then I'd won.' *Lou Reed*

'*Rock And Roll Heart* is very danceable, the kind of thing that if you were sitting in a bar, and either wanted to punch somebody or fuck, you'd probably play it on the juke box. The single will probably be "Banging On My Drum", that's what the Ramones should do. Three chords is three chords, but there is a finesse to it.' *Lou Reed*

'One kid said to me, he really liked the lyrics to "Banging On My Drum", and I said but there are no lyrics to "Banging On My Drum". But he said "FRUSTRATION". I thought I'd written a song about having lots of fun, fun, fun. But apparently not. *Rolling Stone* said that song was all about masturbation – so that just goes to show.' *Lou Reed*

'When I heard the tape of "Temporary Thing" I thought, "Oh no Lou you're right on the edge". You know I really play for keeps. I've got more energy now, I know just where to put it. My band is really good now, there's nothing to be done about it, it's just the nature of the beast.' *Lou Reed*

'There's a good line in "Senselessly Cruel": "Now the time has come to lay to waste/The theory that people have of getting an acquired taste." You either have taste or you don't. You can't acquire it.' *Lou Reed*

'The thing is, my records are for real, but that song "I Believe In Love", from *Rock And Roll Heart* – coming from Lou Reed that is supposed to be a very peculiar statement.' *Lou Reed*

'I don't sit down and say I've got to write a song. I don't do anything about it. I just stay out of the way. Sometimes something will stick with me, but usually I know that if I stick something down on cassette I will only re-write it, so that's a lot of wasted energy. I had a couple of songs before we went into the studio to record *Rock And Roll Heart*, but they changed. The rest I wrote in the studio, it's much more fun that way. It isn't expensive, I'm very quick. It took 27 days to record that album, including mixing. It took as long to mix as it took to record. *Rock And Roll Heart* is very well produced, though I do say so myself.' *Lou Reed*

'This waiter came up to me in a restaurant and said, "Listen, I write songs, what do you suggest I do?" I said, "Let me hear them so I can steal them off you if there's anything good".' *Lou Reed*

'I used to dream in colour, a sign of a high IQ. Every once in a while I'd dream up a fantastic title like *Rock And Roll Heart*.' *Lou Reed*

'Rock'n'roll's not supposed to have lyrics printed on the back, but there are fanatics who believe my lyrics word for word, things which are just impossible. I still don't know the lyrics to *Rock And Roll Heart* – I make them up as I go along.' *Lou Reed*

Rock And Roll Heart *was released to mixed reviews in October 1976, confounding most people's expectations.*

'Certainly don't bother with this record unless, that is, you're the kind of person that gets off on watching paint dry. Come to think of it, *Rock And Roll Heart* would make the perfect background music for that.' *Nick Kent, New Musical Express*

'It's the closest to my mind that Lou Reed's ever got to fulfilling his major ambition, ie becoming Andy Warhol.' *Giovanni Dadomo, Sounds*

'*Rock And Roll Heart* will be backed with a tour, a fully-fledged attack, a seething assault, I call it germ warfare. I like to think of us as the Clearasil on the face of the nation. Jim Morrison would have said that if he was smart, but he's dead.' *Lou Reed*

He then toured America, flanked on stage each night by a bank of fifty TV sets. Even though the shows were billed as 'An evening with a Rock

LOU REED HAS ALWAYS BEEN ABLE TO REFLECT THE LIFE GOING ON AROUND HIM IN HIS SONGS.

OUIS

« Il n'y a qu'un Lou Reed », dit
Lou Reed. Et c'est lui, bien sûr,
lunatique personnage qui traque
la presse jusqu'au fin fond des
bars d'Amérique – pour répondre à
des questions qu'on ne lui a
pas posées – puis lui claque
furieusement la porte au
nez. Il n'y a qu'un Lou Reed...

ANNULÉ

s rendu
on. Un
ers moi
Lawson
« Street
pondre :
enversa
tions là,
critique
er inter-
ce que
résenter,
liste qui

as es-
Street
n pré
n'Ro
i-là, j'
né, de
ridicule
ttendu
is épa
cesseu
dialect
autr

Tout commença à aller mieux dans ce bar
de New York où Arista avait jugé bon de
procéder à un rapide briefing avant notre
mission. Car ça ne s'annonçait pas si
bien, pour ne pas dire plutôt mal. La
veille, à Minneapolis, la sono avait explo-
sé au beau milieu de « Sweet Jane ». Fou
de rage, Lou avait démoli tout le matériel,
jeté les amplis du haut de la scène et
expédié ce faisant deux filles à l'hôpital.
Demain soir, il essayait une nouvelle
amplification à Philadelphie, et d'ici-là,
toutes les interviews étaient ANNULÉES.
Je ne pus m'empêcher d'exploser de rire.
Annulées ! Ça commençait à ressembler

branlantes et... hideux, on vous dit. Sou-
riant, Lou Reed s'avance et procède lui-
même aux présentations. Allan Jones, du
« Melody Maker », est salué d'un toni-
truant : « Ah ! Voici le nain syphilitique ! »
Arrivé à moi, Lou jette : « Et ça, c'est le
Français, mon Dieu, comment ai-je
deviné ? » L'athmosphère est à l'eupho-
rie. Les yeux brillants, Lou nous invite à
interviewer le frigo, qui offre ses der-
nières Heineken. Je me retourne à la re-
cherche d'un décapsuleur pour me retrou-
ver nez à nez avec Lou. « Comment as-tu
trouvé le concert ? » « J'ai adoré la sono. »
« Quoi ? » « La sono ! » « Pardon ? » « La
PA, enfin ! » « Non, mon vieux. Tu as
...SON

**PUBLICITY FOR *ROCK AND ROLL HEART*, LOU REED'S
FIRST ALBUM FOR ARISTA.**

---

*And Roll Heart', Lou's jazz-tinged sound was
augmented by occasional appearances from jazz
trumpeter Don Cherry. Meanwhile, Lou's former record company made moves to cash-in on
the performer's high profile by releasing the* Walk
On The Wild Side *compilation album.*

'I didn't tour for two years, 'cos there was
no reason to, no reason to put out that kind
of energy. I felt in a sense that I'd made a
mistake doing it in public. I thought, "Yeah,

I'm happy sitting in a room playing around
with my guitar." I didn't think I needed all
those hassles, so I stopped dead, I didn't
touch the guitar, but I got lucky and met
Clive Davis, now I'm out there with guys
playing my way. It's no back-up band, we've
been playing together a long time, but it's
my band and it's real. There's a solo on
"Ladies Pay" that's an incredible guitar solo,
it's not even a solo, it's a part. My horn
player does it live but I did it in the studio.
It's almost evil the way it goes past, it's like a
sound wave – I mean it's right back to the
stuff in the Velvets.' *Lou Reed*

'I don't like conventional light shows. I think
my monitors are more colourful. Colour you
see normally, but black and white you don't.
So black and white is colour. It has an effect
because there's no greys. I'm bringing the
monitors on tour in Europe.' *Lou Reed*

'Weren't those TVs fabulous though. Depending on where you sit and how long you've been there soon you see the whole rack blooming. I hope the audience has a good time.' *Lou Reed*

Reed planned to take the show to Europe in 1977. However, with Britain in the throws of the punk rock explosion – and with Lou widely referred to as the godfather of punk – he was prevented from playing the kind of venues he'd singled out for his highly visual show – like the London Palladium. The tour went ahead . . . but without the TVs.

'My current designation as godfather of punk is shit, ridiculous, I'm too literate to be into punk rock. The Ramones are cute, but I don't really know anything about punk rock. I don't think I'm responsible for anything. The whole CBGBs, New Max's thing that everyone's into – and what's going on in London – you don't seriously think

Alive and pumping *Rock n' Roll Heart* LOU REED

Album ARTY 142
Cass TC ARTY 142
ARISTA His debut album on Arista.

I'm responsible for what's mostly rubbish.' *Lou Reed*

'A punk is a misplaced hippy.' *Lou Reed*

'I wanted to play the London Palladium, but they don't want me. They say, "Lou Reed, isn't he something to do with punk?" And they don't want me. But I'd like to play there because it's the right size. I'd like to play a cathedral as well. That would be just nice. In my stage act I use 60 television sets. Video. They're punk art. Snotty punk art.' *Lou Reed*

'I'm on the way to Stockholm where the temperature is below zero. But it's much colder in the heart of the person that banned me. Even Judy Garland couldn't get banned at the Palladium. England is the Achilles heel of Europe.' *Lou Reed*

'I'm so tired of the theory of the noble

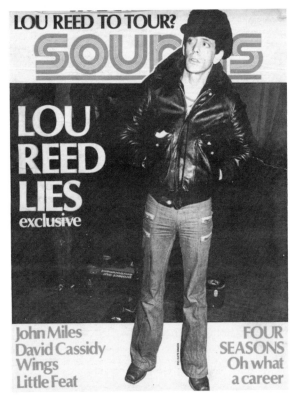

LOU REED TO TOUR?
SOUNDS
LOU REED LIES
exclusive

John Miles
David Cassidy
Wings
Little Feat

FOUR SEASONS
Oh what a career

A TALK ON THE MILD SIDE

r a man who, only two years ago, was
eading the list of potential rock'n'
ll casualties, and drawing critical
uquets along the lines of "...probab-
y the most burnt-out ghostly hunk of
sted talent that still has the nerve
 stagger on stage" and "...a panderer
iving off the dumbbell nihilism of a
Os generation that doesn't have the
ergy to commit suicide", Lou Reed is
 pretty good shape
 Both the voice and the handshake are
rm, and the appearance - after several
ears of coming on like a human chamel-
on loaded up with a frightening var-
ty of hormones - has reverted to a
ose kinship with his photo in the inn-
 sleeve of the first Velvets album.
 The mind seems to have recovered some
 the incisiveness and alertness that
ere once the first things to be assoc-
ted with it, and...are my eyes deceiv-
g me??...the man actually smiles quite
lot. A rather private, distant smile,
 t a smile nonetheless.
 The only problem is that Lou is tired.
 the end of two days of interviews he
 just about reached the end of his
 ., and as he spends most of his
 back in his chair and yawning,
 is less than a triumph in
 ication.
 le his excuses and left,
 ne Arista press officer,
 his is due entirely to
 ses to try and rearr-
 ing Lou's tour of Bri-

 use the dialogue
 er all, it's some
 d a Lou Reed in-
 'd in the
 etc.etc.
 esting
 ws how
 nter-
 the

THE RELEASE OF *ROCK AND ROLL HEART* COINCIDED WITH THE PUNK EXPLOSION IN THE UK AND LOU REED'S UNWELCOME ACCOLADE AS THE GODFATHER OF PUNK.

Nelson Slater's 'Wild Angels'.

Who's he?

Nelson Slater?...he's a friend of mine
that I produced..

Is he another guy from New York?

No, he's San Francisco.

*When did you do that...I never heard
about it?*

I didn't do it as well as David did Iggy
I suppose..

Was it a recent project?

It was right after 'Coney Island Baby'.

And did the album actually get a release?

I think RCA released it to about three
people.

*Where did you meet the particular guys
in your new band (Michael Fonfara -
Keyboards; Bruce Yaw - Bass; Michael
Suchorsky - Drums; Marty Fogel - Sax.)*

Fonfara's been with me for quite a while
and the rest have just been there.

*Isn't there another guitarist in the
band apart from yourself?*

Yeah...aaarrgggh!oooeeeoooh!...just releasing my tensions and inhibitions! Yes,
I've got another guitar player...every-
body in the band is the same as on the
album except I've added another guitar
player...I have augmented the band with
one more six-string electric guitar.

And who is he?

His name is Geoffrey.

Geoffrey Somebody or Somebody Geoffrey?

Just Geoffrey...he's only just joined
the band, and if he doesn't work out I
don't want people to know his last name.

*How did you actually meet these players?
Did you find them in New York?*

They just...well, most of them are from
Jersey, as a matter of fact. They just
kind of filtered through.

(The banal line of questioning pursued
thus far is usually a good way of open-

ing an interview. It gives the interviewer a chance to get himself relaxed
without having to pay close attention
to the answers, because he should know
them already, and most artists are only
to happy to extol the virtues of their
current backing group. Lou's reluctance
to give even the most basic information
augurs badly.)

*Do you normally meet your backing groups
by accident, then? How about The Tots?
(Lou's group while he was here in '78.)*

Yeah. They just happened to be running
around...which they probably still are,
just laying there...except I'm sure
they're no longer called The Tots.
Benny was 17...a good guitar player.

*It was that extrovert bass player that
I remember best from that band...*
(A little reminiscence of this nature
can often provoke the interviewee to
respond with some of his own...a funny
anecdote,perhaps, or a recollection with
some particular relevance.)

He was an animal.
(It doesn't always work, though.)

*Do you tend to pick up ready-made bands,
or do you put them together?*

No, not ready-made.

Not even the Tots?

Well, the Tots were a group, basically.
(Lou seems to find the subject of musicians that he has worked with to be an
uninteresting topic of conversation. A
change of tack is called for...)

*There seems to be a change in your song-
writing on the new album...an emphasis
on the musical rather than the lyrical
side...*

I think that's true.

Is there any particular reason for that?

I got all the players in. On 'Coney Island Baby' I was missing two of them, so
I couldn't do it at the time. For 'Rock
'n'Roll Heart' we got 'em all in, so I
changed the songs to match that.

But you had a full complement of players

on 'Berlin',
phasis is cer

Well, that wa
wasn't with a

So Coney Isla
like your fir
apart from th

Absolutely.

*Was that a di
take when you
had you decid
such for a wh
people?*

That was a co
a 'band band'
musicians.

*What...a come
Island Baby,
leaving the V
long time to*

When I left t
what I wanted
I wanted to h

*Was there any
that change i*

Well, it's ju
can do it by
do what I war
by myself. I
just individu
...it's gotta

*Was that a de
Can't Dance',
Lou isn't goi
his own accor
interviewer t
controversy.)*

Yeah well, it
particularly
sucks. That w
I don't like
was on that a
ed with him,

*Several of th
been in your*

Oh.

*So where did
the last two
successful?*

Well, it has
kinds of thir
ships, the we
the way they
pathetic towe
...you gotta

*Surely th-
expert?*

It w

---

savage. I'd like to hear punks who weren't at
the mercy of their own rage, and who could
put together a coherent sentence. I mean
they can get away with "Anarchy In The
UK" and all that bullshit, but it hasn't the
intelligence of something like Garland
Jeffreys' *Wild In The Streets.'* Lou Reed, in
support of an old friend

*Having endured consistant problems with the
press over the years, Lou was clearly disen-
chanted by the enthusiasm that greeted the punk
scene – at the expense of any media interest in his
work.*

'It's been a long time since I spoke to any
journalists. This afternoon I've been interviewed twice. Now I remember why I gave
up speaking to journalists, they are a species
of foul vermin. I mean I wouldn't hire

Melody Maker

DECEMBER 11, 1976   15p weekly   USA 75 cents

ETHRO
O TOUR

ARISTA

PUNKS: WHAT NEXT?–P4

**McGarrigles, Harper
on the road again**

**Lou Reed,
Godfather
of punk, in
MM next week**

93

rock & folk

N° 140

lou reed,
genesis, pete
townshend
interviews

dico
disco

people like you to guard my sewer. Journalists are morons, idiots. Journalists are ignorant and stupid. Journalists wear you down by sheer drudgery, it's beyond blind persistence. You can hit them, stab them, kick them in the shins, abuse them and outrage them and they won't even notice.' *Lou Reed*

'It doesn't give me pleasure to be bitchy when I'm not in a bitchy mood, but if I'm in a bitchy mood I'll bitch. Then if it progresses to the bastardly mood, then to the prick mood, then I'll be pricky about it. Then if it goes past there, it's every man for himself.' *Lou Reed*

'Nixon was beautiful, if he had bombed Montana and gotten away with it, I would have loved him. I have no fear . . . of anything.' *Lou Reed*

'Sometimes performing as Lou Reed and being Lou Reed are so close as to make one think that they are one and the same person. I've hidden behind the myth of Lou Reed for years. I can blame anything outrageous on him. I make believe sometimes that I am Lou Reed. I'm so easily seduced by the

public image of Lou Reed, that I'm in love with Lou Reed myself. I think he's wonderful. Sometimes I just like being Lou Reed better than I like being anyone else.' *Lou Reed*

'Unintentionally the Velvets have become something of a spectre, I'd have to agree with that. Songs like "Heroin" and "Waiting For The Man" are not easily forgotten – you are constantly judged by songs like that. I still do them. You know, we were rehearsing yesterday – much to everyone's surprise we do rehearse – and we were running through "Waiting For The Man", y' know, 26 dollar in my hand, and I said, "Hey wait a minute 26 dollars?" I mean you can't even get a blow job for 26 dollars these days, let alone get some smack. So we were all saying, "Jesus Christ, what's the going price these days? Somebody get out on the street and find out. It can't be 26 dollars." Y'know, we wanted to be authentic. Eventually we decided that the song would have to be classified under folk mystique because we couldn't find out. Anyway the song isn't outdated, everything about that song holds true, except the price.' *Lou Reed*

'I know that half these people turn up at my concerts to see if I'm going to drop dead on stage, and they're so disappointed that I'm still around and writing and capable of performing without falling down and stumbling around. But I haven't OD'd. And I know that a whole mess of those people would have been just ecstatic if five years ago I'd have OD'd, then the legend for them would have been complete.' *Lou Reed*

'They wanted me to OD and they never even gave me the dope to do it with. They even expected me to do it with my own dope. Anyway I'm not into dope, that's true, why are you laughing? I don't smoke grass and I don't like things that everyone sniffs off a table. That's tawdry, it's so common, I like to play with my own system, alone. I'm

he Avatar
f Decay
ies With
he Dead

Reed

rsmith Odeon

week was
riate. Lou Reed
to rise from the
very few years, and
he brought his
rs with him.

epileptic Frankenstein's
monster. Most of all I hated
the way that, with a few
imperious waves of his podgy
arm, he had all the
photographers hustled from
the front of the stage during
his third number.

"I've never like journalists
and photographers," he

Belushi. It was *baaad*. A
later 'Perfect Day' was
savaged by Reed's path
attempt to sing falsetto
Apparently, he's been
listening to The Isley Br
Gosh, Lou, and I'd thou
Wanna Be Black' was a

Things improved
dramatically with a stro
lean version of 'Men Of
Fortune', followed by th
whole of side two of 'Be
The band were suitably
restrained, Reed seeme
involved with his singin
the stark power of those
songs was overwhelmi
Then he blew it by
underselling 'Street Ha
a comedy item.

The encore was little
than an insult.

'Bells', from the new
lurched from one
interminable crescendo
another, with Reed offs
for most of the time. Th
few bars of 'Rock And R
segued into a histrionic
Keep Me Hanging On'
by the bass player — wl
went on and on and *on*
ON. Everyone took a so
Everyone took anoth
The sax player d
laboured Coltr
drummer re
of Ginger F

Peopl
gum

figure from the bozo zone? Pic PENNIE SMITH.

es on
ast

g

and phrasing exactly right.
But when he tried to *sing*, a
tortured croak was all that
came out and this was
promptly stomped on h
hand.

excr

**LOU REED FALLS FOUL OF THE BRITISH PRESS – AGAIN
– ON HIS 1979 TOUR.**

into drug masturbation.' *Lou Reed*

'I didn't even feel sorry for Jim Morrison
when he died. I remember there was a
group of us sitting in this apartment in New
York and the telephone rang and someone
told us that Jim Morrison had just died in
a bathtub in Paris. And the immediate
reaction was, "How fabulous, in a bathtub,
in Paris, how *faaaantastic*." That lack of
compassion doesn't disturb me at all, he
asked for it. I had no compassion at all for

You're out of
ime my baby

REED
amersmith

E'S A line in one of
songs Lou, that
es the mockery I
he other night:
s a bum trip". And
xactly what it was,

that vein, the glory would
have been his. As it is, the
press will have a field
day. Lou Reed Flops
Again, what more can
anyone ask?

'Waiting For The Man'
was tediously dr
and slowed
crowd were
among the

in the past. For Chr'
sake we're going int
eighties and y
singing songs th
alm

95

LOU REED: NO MORE HEROES, BUT PLENTY OF RESPECT
by Billy Altman

> " I'm too much of a smartass...I knew Bruce (Springsteen) would do it seriously.

One of the words mentioned most often in regard to Lou Reed's work is *honest* so I may as well start this story with a confession. I met Lou Reed once before I talked to him on the verge of *Street Hassle*'s release. It was in 1972; a small and devoted bunch of us rock 'n' roll crazies had taken over our college's concert committee and up being Reed's very first gig as a solo artist. It meant a lot to us that he was going to play two nights in the enchanting Millard Fillmore Room on the campus of the University of Buffalo. The one and only time that I'd seen the Velvet Underground live was during their final glorious stand at Max's Kansas City two summers previous, and that show affected me more than any other concert I'd ever seen before.

And now here he was in town. The day after the first show, a few of us wandered over to his motel room to formally meet him. As we walked in, I noticed that he had the local daily newspaper spread out on the bed, open to the page that included a rave review of the show the night before; a rave review that I had written. I felt

[partial text column obscured behind clipping]
a bit awkward about t... we were introduced, th... belonged to me, but I wa... dumbfounded at finally... that it seemed the only... the ice. But Lou just... shoved the paper away, an... "Yeah, always nice to get... in a voice that seemed so c... ing that I was just flattened... about five excruciatingly lo... in his room, with hardly a... said by anyone, and th... Throughout the weekend... curt to the point of obi... with just about everyone... I stood in the back of the h... him play the second nigh... very first new band of his... from the suburbs. He was... uptight, rigid and tentati... that a whole slew of thoug... my mind concerning a... lationship to himself and... If the Lou Reed we'd met... tenth as interesting as th... we'd been idolizing on re... these years, did it take av... from our feelings about... Moreover, if the Lou Reed... that night seemed to be... away from the Lou Reed I'c... whelmed by that night a... that affect my opinions... vious work? When I rea... answer to both questio... occurred to me that I ha... really thought of my favo... as *human beings*, and... that they were like th... something I'd be doin... that day on. I guess I w... So there I was at... restaurant in midtov... waiting for Lou Reed to... interview (he was alrea... hours late), and rem... things past such as the... through my head. I wa... I'd heard a cassette c... and that old fire se... finally been rekindled... transcendant collectio... just had it, y'know. I... first album for RCA an... *Baby*, I didn't care m... solo stuff—maybe a... there, like "Satellite O... Your Sons"— but, li... people with roughly t... bilities as me, each ne... bring that brief spar... before you played it... time he'd really do it... That my expecta... raised in regard to S... mostly a result of see... summer at the Botto... dine-packed showc...

36

that silly Los Angeles person. How dumb, he was *so* dumb. If he was around today, they'd be saying the same things about him as they're saying about me.' *Lou Reed*

'I'm interested in myself. My writing hasn't changed, once you've attained perfection, what else can you do? Kiss me and I'll be nice. Otherwise look out.' *Lou Reed*

'You've gotta be careful with guys like Reed.' *Tom Verlaine*

'The minute I start getting reviews saying I'm tasteful, I'm gonna shoot myself. How dare anyone call rock'n'roll tasteful.' *Lou Reed*

'I hate downers, people get sloppy like drunks. I don't like marijuana, that's for sure, just the smell of it – and it's so commercial. It just makes you hungry. It's just like cartoons, and LSD is like bigger cartoons. I don't like to get high, because what I'm saying may not be what's there. You discover the universal truth in four hours,

MIRROR, MIRROR ON THE WALL! WHO IS THE GREATEST ROCK STAR OF ALL?

They all said I was past it, finished, but I proved those stoopid faggots wrong. I'm back, man, better than ever I was, if that's possible. I'm still the greatest. Who else is there? Nobody, man. Everybody wants me for interviews, I don't mind 'cos I love talkin' about myself, and the brainless cretins who buy records have finally realised that I'm the only one worth listenin' to. Johnny Rotten, who's he? Bruce Springsteen? His songs just ain't

THANKS GUYS, YOU'VE BEEN A PERFECT AUDIENCE!

worthwhile, they ain't about me so they can't be. I'm so hot, man, that every time I touch my guitar I get burnt. Then again, our faggot of a roadie was never very good at electrics. I don't need audience applause, man. I get my thrills lookin' in the mirror. I just need my own applause. I'm a songwriter 'cos I love words......especially words like , me, I, myself, mine......................

the village VOICE

Copyright© 1978
The Village Voice   VOL. XXIII No. 12   THE WEEKLY NEWSPAPER OF NEW YORK   MARCH 20, 1978   60¢

Lou Reed Reads Runes

By Susin Shapiro

STEPHANIE CHERNIKOWSKI

You think maybe Lou wants to be a superstar?

A funny thing happened to Milton on the way to Paradise. He discovered the devils to be more fascinating than the angels, and that gave him hell. Lou Reed has also been prey to ᵗʰ problems. His new album, *Street Hassle,* is up to its ᵈᵉᵛils. But at last Reed has introduced them to his ⁿᵉ good times/gimme ʰᵃⁿt of both *Street* ᵉʳʳies the same ʳᵉ exorcised ᵈ has jug- ᵒⁿs, but ᵗᵉs and

forget it in the fifth, and in the sixth you're hungry. You see strawberries walking across the ceiling, and then what else is there? Quaaludes make me a maniac, they make me very nervous. I don't think it is normal to slow yourself down.' *Lou Reed*

'My idea of relaxing is playing. When that becomes like work, is when I take a walk. Playing is my relaxation, travelling is a drag. There's only one thing I like playing – rock'n'roll to rock'n'roll musicians. I didn't

jᵐ ' ᵒⁿ Onstage he's puckish, like Chaplin, like the ⁿᵈ *Baby,* a live highlight. He moves like a ᵛardly, authentically, uncorrupteᵈ ʰ ⁿⁿa Be Black," b ᵉ like Malcoᵗ

want to be a jazz musician, didn't want to do classical, didn't want to ever work. I've never worked. Whenever it looked like something was happening like work, I'd do something to stop it. I play rock'n'roll and that's it. That's all I've ever wanted to do, and that's what I do.' *Lou Reed*

97

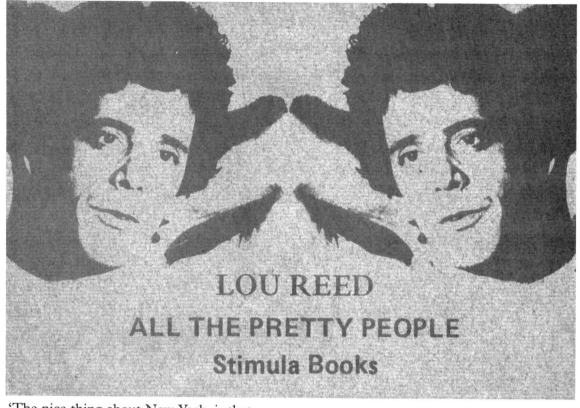

LOU REED
ALL THE PRETTY PEOPLE
Stimula Books

'The nice thing about New York, is that you're anonymous, I mean, who wants to be known?' *Lou Reed*

A RARE LIMITED EDITION BOOKLET OF STARK AND BRUTAL POETRY.

After an intense period of recording and live activity (he'd recorded and promoted nine albums in the five years between 1972 and 1976) Lou was due a break and, by his standards, 1977 was a quiet year. He was also at the end of his long-term relationship with Rachel, and trying to get his life together – again. However, by late 1977 Lou was already showcasing numbers with the same band as Rock And Roll Heart, *which would soon appear on his* Street Hassle *album (released in 1978), which would be recorded using the revolutionary – but ill fated – binaural sound system. Co-produced by Lou Reed and Richard Robinson, the musicians on the album included Stuart Heinrich (guitar), Marty Fogel (saxophone) and Michael Suchorsky (drums). Lou toured the States in the Spring of that year, during which time he played a series of memorable dates at New York's*

Bottom Line Club – recorded for the Take No Prisoners *live package. At this time Lou also received a reward from the American Literary Council of Little Magazines, who recognised him as one of the year's top five new poets. Lou responded in a typically perverse manner by promptly cancelling the publication of his first collection of verse,* All The Pretty People.

'Note for note, Street Hassle is exactly what it's supposed to be. It's not disposable like most records. The situations are real and human, the way Eugene O'Neil might write a song. I wouldn't change a hair on it.' *Lou Reed*

'The new album's a lot of fun – lovely music, very dirty, mainstream snot.' *Lou Reed on the release of* Street Hassle.

RECORDS

Lou Reed fights the law and wins

Street Hassle
Lou Reed
Arista AB 4169

By Tom Carson

NEAR THE BE-
ginning of this bril-
liant new album, Lou
Reed sings: "It's
been a ____ ime
since I've spoken ____
line has a res ____

its literal mean ____
following the br ____
vet Undergrou ____
and half-bake ____
became a trave ____
one of the m ____
nerves of our ti ____
a crude, death-t ____

Whereas Re ____
vets had once ____
with a compell ____
and redemptio ____
them by tur ____
Underground ____
freak shows. ____
Reed's solo wo ____
bad, one has ____
admirers ____
Bob D ____
had ____
e ____

LOU REED — STREET HASSLE

LOU REED STREET HASSLE

ON ARISTA RECORDS AND TAPES

'I like my trash to sound better than any-body else's trash, because I make records to sell records. It's an enormously commercial album. I feel right in step with the market, I like to think that we're going to hit the curve at the same time. My audience always knows that they're going to get a Lou Reed record for better or worse. The direction might change but it's always going to bear my stamp.' *Lou Reed*

'Nobody could possibly take "I Wanna Be Black" seriously. My producer said that no good would come of this, but the idea of getting shot in the spring, like Martin Luther King, is hysterically funny to me.' *Lou Reed*

'Nobody wants to be a rhythm guitarist anymore except niggers. You know that Marvin Gaye song, "Gotta Give It Up", the album version? When Marvin says, "here comes the good part" – it's the truth. That rhythm guitarist, his throwaways are riffs that people would give their left ball for. I tried to do that kind of guitar on "I Wanna Be Black". Naturally I fucked it up, but that's my attempt to do Ed Brown.' *Lou Reed*

'When Clive [Davis] heard the original "Street Hassle" track, which is two minutes and eleven seconds long, he said that it was great and that I should make it longer. So I

AN AMERICAN LITERARY MAGAZINE INCLUDED LOU'S AWARD WINNING POETRY.

THE COLDSPRING JOURNAL

vivà
aram saroyan
lou reed

did. "Street Hassle" is basically a two minute-odd tape loop. The basic track's all the same, but with different overdubs put over it. It shows how many ways you can look at the same thing. What I did was record a whole string section but I only used part of it – the cello. I only brought in the whole string section for one part, so it kind of sweeps in real panoramic. I had three vignettes, so I thought the perfect thing here was to dissolve, like in a movie – shift one set of music past another set, sort of pan them and BOOM! you're into the second world.' *Lou Reed*

Bruce Springsteen was invited to provide additional vocals on Street Hassle, *since he happened to be in New York's Record Plant Studios at the same time.*

'Bruce [Springsteen] was mixing in the studio below us and I thought, how fortuitous, let's get Bruce. People expect me to bad-mouth him because he's from New Jersey, but I think he's really fabulous. He did the part so well that I had to bury him in the mix.' *Lou Reed*

'*Street Hassle* is recorded on a system that will probably revolutionise all recordings. It's called binaural. All you need is a cheap pair of headphones, and you just plug it into anything and you'll hear a 360 sound. There is no stereo, there's no left or right, it's total. You've never heard anything like it in your life. And it is spectacular. The stuff on the new album is amazing, it really is right down there, kinda rock. It's been a long time since I really got down there.' *Lou Reed*

'When we were in Montreal, before we went on someone in the audience was yelling, "Take no prisoners Lou – SMACK" – then the guy would just bash his head against the table. "Lou Reed take no prisoners – SMACK". I thought the phrase was great, it couldn't have been more appropriate, don't take us prisoners, beat us to death, shoot us, mame us, kill us, but don't settle for less, go all the way. That's what I took it to mean.' *Lou Reed*

When Take No Prisoners *first appeared in the UK shops, the album came with a sticker on the cover warning of the controversial nature of Lou's language, and the personal comments contained within the recording.*

'It's funny, but whenever I ask anyone what they think of *Take No Prisoners* they say, "Well I love it, but I'm a little worried about what other people will think." Except one friend, he told me he thought it was very manly, that's admirable. It's like the military maxim the title comes from – give no quarter, take no prisoners – I wanted to make a record that wouldn't give an inch. If anything, it would push the world back just an inch or two. If *Metal Machine Music* was just a "hello" note, *Take No Prisoners* is the letter that should have gone with it. You may find this funny, but I think of it as a contemporary urban blues album, after all, that's what I write, tales of the city. And if I drop dead tomorrow, this is the record that I'd choose for posterity. It's not only the smartest thing I've ever done, it's also as close to Lou Reed as you're ever going to get, for better or for worse.' *Lou Reed*

'In all modesty, I think that's one of the funniest albums made by a human. There was no way you could save that record from not being air-playable. There were so many things, that you just wouldn't know where to start. Which is why I did it in private, and no-one got to hear it till the end. By the time I gave them the album, there was nothing anyone could do, it was just an unfortunate accepted fact. On the other hand though, it was also impossible for anyone to listen to it and not fall over laughing. So, between laughs, they would say to me, "But Lou" . . . So we left it at that. I was thinking of calling the album *But Lou . . .*' *Lou Reed*

BY THE *beginning of 1979, Lou was in reflecti* *mood. Rachel was now out of his life for go* *and, at the age of 37, the artist was more the* *ready to set his house in order. Professionally,* *was in the process of completing work on T* Bells.

'I've had more of a chance to make an asshole out of myself than most people, an I realise that. But then not everybody gets the chance to live out their nightmares for the vicarious pleasures of the public.' *Lou Reed*

'I believe in all things in moderation – including moderation. I did more than abuse my body in the past, I very often wounded it. I enjoy age, I was miserable when I was younger.' *Lou Reed*

Lou Reed Live (What, Agai The Audience As Hostage

Lou Hon, who certainly of the quantitative aspect o roll (and seems to have fisted grasp on Eliot's co that poetry [correlate free a turning loose of emotio expression of personali rather an escape from t simply fueling the enigmati that wheels him through tory where the good shit bad shit fuse, creating fr varication and integrity, pa intensity and profound indi a—to again cop from terrible beauty that reje ludicrous notions of Best o of genius or idiocy, of dark light. And if Reed *is* aloo consummate knowing, t preceding the ones quote in "The Second Coming think, gaze a steady beam nature of his rock 'n' roll: "The blood-dimmed tide is and everywhere ᵐony of inn⌐

The Great White Hope

versus

The Thin White Duke

'I use my moods. I get into one of these dark melancholy things and I just milk it for everything I can. I know I'll be out of it soon, and that I won't be looking at things the same way. But for every dark mood, I also have a euphoric opposite. I think they say that manic depressives go as high as they go down, which isn't to say that I'm really depressive.' *Lou Reed*

'You take the lyric and you push it a little forward so that it speaks to you on a personal level and still keeps the beat, because I'm not talking about poetry reading. You can even make it a dialogue between men and women. That could keep you occupied for the rest of your life.' *Lou Reed*

'My expectations are very high . . . to be the greatest writer that ever lived on God's earth. In other words I'm talking about Shakespeare, Dostoevsky. I want to do that rock'n'roll thing that's on the level of *The Brothers Karamazov* . . . starting to build up a body of work. I'm on the right track. I think I haven't done badly. But I think I haven't really scratched the surface. I think I'm just starting.' *Lou Reed*

'Usually I can't read my own hand-writing. I had it analysed and they couldn't even read it to analyse it. It's like the bank when they take your signature to match against cheques. They have ten signatures for me. They said they just needed one, to protect me . . . from myself?' *Lou Reed*

Throughout 1978 and 1979, Lou gave several candid interviews regarding his sexuality. These were either spawned by the drink or speed which fuelled him to talk more readily than usual, or simply by the fact that the gay issue did come to a head in New York at this time. Ironically the new decade would see him enter a second marriage.

THE MUSIC PRESS WAS DELIGHTED BY THE REPORTED SCRAP BETWEEN DAVID BOWIE AND LOU REED AT A LONDON RESTAURANT IN 1979.

Rolling Stone

March 22nd, 1979 • Issue No. 287

Lou Reed's heart of darkness

face, masked with a poised, distant
expression, looks wo... But h...
hind that lurid veil l...
fitful psyche, and
ounces of bourbon
it can be virulen...

Lou has be...
an hour a...
Take No...
double li...
ics as his...

April 6-12 1979 No.468

Time Out

Guitars by Guitar Man

sunglasses by Ray-Ban

leather jacket by Schott

head-phone by Yam...

make up by...

Now

Lou Reed.
Which face will the Godfather
of punk show London this time?
Exclusive interview inside.

'I have such a heavy resentment thing because of all the prejudices against me being gay. How can anybody gay keep their sanity? Sometimes I feel like getting a gun out and shooting people, but there would be so many people to shoot.' *Lou Reed*

'Being gay I have found that so many women, deluded creatures that they are, are attracted to you because you're not interested in them. Granted I'm Lou Reed, and I have all this access, but even before I was Lou Reed it happened that way. I could walk in and, just because I wasn't interested, it came across as the ultimate cool. "Hey, he really doesn't give a shit". It never dawned on anybody that he doesn't give a shit because he couldn't. I think women most appreciate men who ultimately don't need them. A lot of women get very tired of being needed.' *Lou Reed*

The late seventies saw an increasing level of bad feeling levied at New York's gay community. In an attempt to nullify some of the restrictions placed upon this minority group, a Gay Rights bill was presented for approval under State law. When it was turned down, Lou was outspoken in his condemnation of the bureaucrats' decision.

'I'm very disturbed about that council vote defeating the Gay Rights bill. I'd just come out of seeing *Halloween*, which was a really great movie and I ran into a gay rally in Times Square the day after the vote. Because they didn't pass the Gay Rights bill, if you're gay you can't get access to federal housing under New York State law. I can't help but, at times, take it very very very *very* seriously. It's so maddening to me, I become incapable of lucid thought.' *Lou Reed*

'I just wouldn't want listeners to be under a false impression. I want them to know, if they're liking a man, that it's a gay one, from top to bottom.' *Lou Reed*

'Rock'n'roll is a great equaliser, I love rock'n'roll, I honest to God do. I like feeling that fucking drum.' *Lou Reed*

In spite of these protestations, Lou's new album was to have much more of a jazz feel to it – as songs written with Nils Lofgren were augmented by the involvement of trumpeter Don Cherry. Lou also wrote three songs for Nils Lofgren which appeared on the latter's Nils *album. These were 'A Fool Like Me', 'I Found Her' and 'I'll Cry Tomorrow'.*

'I wrote some of the songs with Nils Lofgren. We got together with Bob Ezrin and wrote some really good things together. It's gonna be a big sound, with various machines making the guitar sound like a symphony. It'll be so grand. I'm gonna produce it myself, what the hell. I know it can be done on stage, and the show will get more fantastic. I have more plans regarding video, we're going into colour. I work on that very hard.' *Lou Reed*

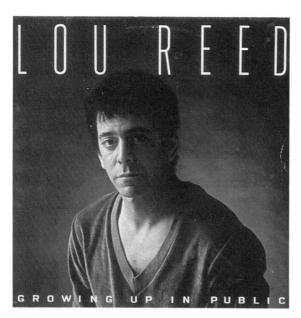

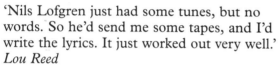

'Nils Lofgren just had some tunes, but no words. So he'd send me some tapes, and I'd write the lyrics. It just worked out very well.' *Lou Reed*

'Most of the other songs were co-written with the band, which is something I haven't done since the Velvets.' *Lou Reed*

Lou Reed's act of love

A nation of rock & roll hearts

The Bells
Lou Reed
Arista

By Lester Bangs

EVERYBODY ALWAYS talks about the poor homeless orphan waifs, but what about the homeless fathers? The time has come to call the fathers home from the stale curbstone shores. Sometimes they're bad and *Take No Prisoners*. But who then do they finally hurt but themselves? And when they give of themselves, they reaffirm what great art has always been: an act of love toward the whole human race. Then it becomes time to give at least a little love back.

Lou Reed is a prick and a jerkoff who regularly commits the ultimate sin of treating his audience with contempt. He's also a person with deep compassion for a great many other people about whom almost nobody else gives a shit. I won't say who they are, because I don't want to get too schmaltzy, except to emphasize that there's always been more to this than drugs and fashionable kinks, and to point out that suffering, loneliness and psychic/spiritual exile are great levelers.

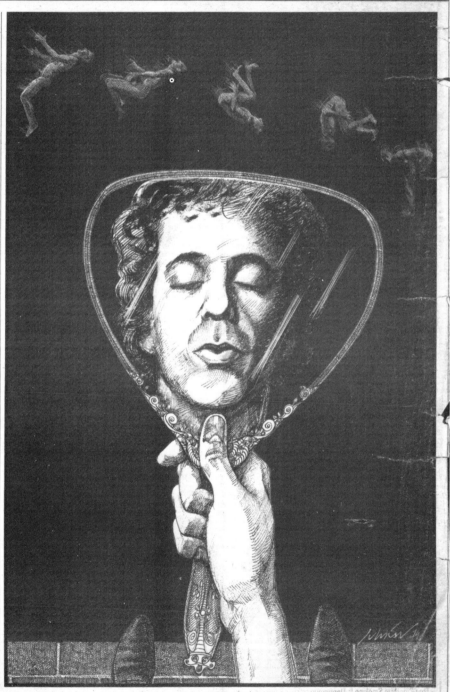

The Bells *was released in March 1979. Produced by Bob Ezrin, it was recorded just outside Hamburg. The core of the band responsible for* Street Hassle *and* Take No Prisoners *were again in force, namely Michael Fonfara (keyboards), Marty Fogel (sax), Ellard Boles (bass) and Michael Suchorsky (drums). A spring tour of Europe followed almost immediately.*

'The Bells is about a suicide, not a bad suicide, but an ecstatic movement. It's a guy who's in love with Broadway, or whatever, and he's on the edge of the building, and he looks out and thinks that he sees a brook, and he says "There are the bells", and as he points, he tumbles over a drum roll, it's beautiful.' *Lou Reed*

'My band's incredible, I like playing in a band. I've always wanted to be in rock'n'roll and play my music and make records of it. You have to play with a band. Not back-up musicians, but a real band. Recording is one thing, and playing live is fabulous.' *Lou Reed*

'The Bells is the only true jazz-rock fusion anybody's come up with since Miles Davis' *On The Corner* period.' *Lester Bangs, journalist*

While on the road in 1979, Lou got into trouble in West (as it then was) Berlin after taking a particular dislike to one member of the audience. After refusing to continue the show until the offending party was removed, Reed was booed by the rest of the audience who then started a riot. The artist was promptly arrested on the spot, blamed personally for £10,000 of damage, and hauled off in a police truck.

'They took me to jail alone. How would you like to get into a van with twelve goose-steppers saying they're going to test your blood? . . . The problem was a bunch of drunken American soldiers. They wanted to have a riot, and they had one.' *Lou Reed*

As if this wasn't enough excitement for one European tour, after the last night of the British leg at Hammersmith Odeon, Lou met up with David Bowie at a West End restaurant. During the meal Bowie reputedly made an offensive remark, prompting Reed to lash out in a violent and irrational manner. It's generally believed that the British star was advising the American to clean-up his act, which coincidentally (perhaps) Reed was about to do. Whether this is true or not, the story made headline news for the rest of the week.

'Yes, I hit him – more than once. It was a private dispute. It had nothing to do with sex, politics or rock'n'roll. I have a New York code of ethics – speak unto others as you would have them speak unto you. In other words, watch your mouth.' *Lou Reed*

'There are some severe little tangent things in my songs that remove them from me but, ah yes, they're very personal. I guess the Lou Reed character is pretty close to the real Lou Reed, to the point maybe where there really is no difference between the two – except maybe a piece of vinyl. I keep hedging my bets, instead of saying that's really me. But that is me, as much as you can get on record.' *Lou Reed*

His US dates during this period, as ever, were a much quieter affair. In America he was a cult figure playing small venues. It was Europe where the exposure was – and the money.

'I don't think that people who listen to rock'n'roll for a minute think that the guy who's making music, or singing, is as hip as they are.' *Lou Reed*

Hip or otherwise, his most recent recording work was still a comparative commercial failure.

'Maybe the reason my stuff doesn't have mass appeal, is that it does approach people on a personal level. It assumed a certain agreement of mores, or if not an agreement, then at least an awareness on the listener's part.' *Lou Reed*

'The thing is, I've always tried to do my best to my standards. Every year we put out one or two records, and I always have a great pride that what was ever going down, things were always on time. I'm one of those people that needs a deadline. I like the deadline aspect of it all. I mean, I transpose 12 or 14 lines of poetry within four to six months, to come up with whatever . . . and then it comes out and you've got, say 20 minutes a side. It's like a good pinball game, it's not just luck.' *Lou Reed*

'It's funny, but maybe the most frightening thing that can be said about me is that I'm so damned sane. Maybe these aren't my devils at all that people are finding on these records, maybe they're other people's. When I start writing about my own, then it could

prove really interesting.' *Lou Reed*

To help keep himself sane during this period, Lou bought himself a farm in the New Jersey countryside – staying there whenever he got the opportunity. He also developed an enthusiasm for Chinese boxing!

'I really love the farm, it smells great. Even if you wanted to do something, there's nothing there. It's appalling how much sleep I get. Y'know, Andy used to say you can't see the stars in New York City, because they're all on the ground. Well, out there, the stars are in the sky.' *Lou Reed*

'It's an aesthetic and physical discipline that I find exquisite. The discipline is in the ability to relax. It's very beautiful to watch.' *Lou Reed on Chinese boxing*

'I wouldn't want to be younger. I know more things. I wouldn't want to be eighteen again. When I was eighteen I was really just walking into walls all the time.' *Lou Reed*

By 1980 Lou was living life as a comparative health fanatic, eating wholesome food, enjoying walks in the countryside, and preparing for a substantial new relationship. On 14 February 1980, Lou married the artist and designer, Sylvia Morales, whom he had reputedly met in an S&M club – and who changed his life.

'I think that getting married would be a major influence on anybody's life. I now know that certain things will get taken care of and looked out for just on the home front, and it's on the home front that you can get hurt a lot. It's good to know that you're covered, and beyond just friendship. I'm a great one for commitment. I like to look at centuries past, when knighthood was in flower, I'm still a great one for that. I think I've found my flower, so it makes me feel more like a knight.' *Lou Reed*

'The last thing in the world I would be

interested in doing is blowing it, on a personal health level. I think drugs are the single most terrible thing, and if I thought there was anything I could do which I thought might be effective in stopping

**Well, that's [...]
you say it in [...]
ROTHÉE [...]
the man who [...]
a modern mo[...]**

DL: Is it true that yo[...]
interview was for Vog[...]
after "The Ostrich"? D[...]
remember that?

LOU: My God! How do you [...]
It was a long time ago.

DL: I'd like to know what [...]
when you met Andy Warh[...]
the first time.

LOU: Oh. Well . .

DL: Long time ago . . .

LOU: Seems like only yest[...]
There we were in the M[...]
Rouge. It was a dark night[...]
come by camel. I came [...]
were playing a tourist tra[...]
Greenwich Village called [...]
Bizarre" and some friends [...]
Andy to come down and s[...]
and that he might like t[...]
saw us.

DL: What did he say?

LOU: Oh, he thought [...]
But Andy thinks eve[...]

DL: I know.

LOU: He had a wee[...]
matheque to show h[...]
said, why don't yo[...]
Cinematheque? He [...]
movies on us.

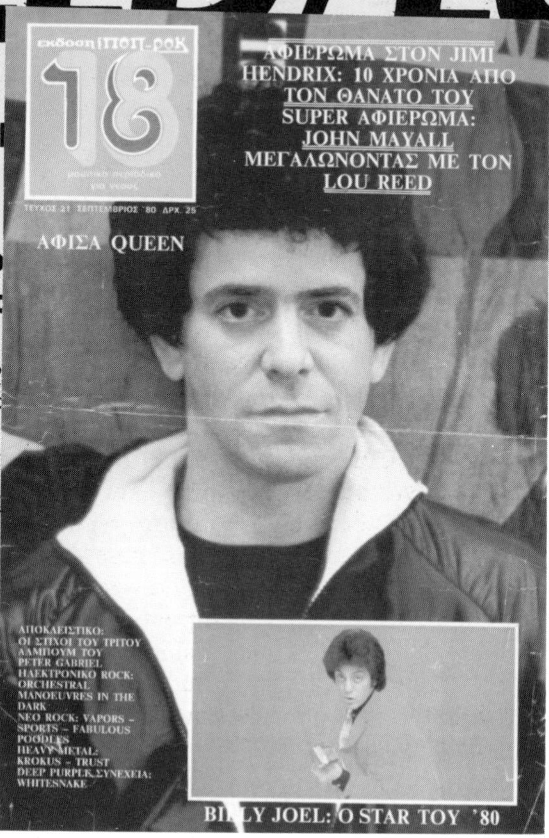

people dealing in drugs, and taking them, I would do it. I just think it's the worst conceivable thing in the world. Before, I didn't care.' *Lou Reed*

'I'm not interested in any morality plays. I just wanted to make it clear to you. I'm not proselytising but, as far as my early demise goes, I've made a lot of efforts in the other direction.' *Lou Reed*

Setting the seal on his new lifestyle, Lou released a watershed album, the confessional Growing Up In Public, *in June 1980. It was the last album he would record in an alcoholic haze, representing – as it did – a real effort to come to terms with the traumas of his past. Put together at George Martin's Montserrat studio, musicians in attendance included Stuart Heinrich (guitar), Chuck Hammer (guitar), Michael Fonfara (keyboards and guitar), Ellard Boles (bass) and Michael Suchorsky (drums). Fonfara also co-produced the work with Reed. The European tour*

of the same year also represented something of a transition, as all drugs were strictly off-limits.

'There are seven million stories in the city. *Growing Up In Public* is all of them.' *Arista promotional tag*

'The album's songs are a composite picture of a certain kind of personality, not necessarily mine.' *Lou Reed*

'*Growing Up In Public* was designed to be as professional as possible. We rehearsed a lot, had everything down before we went in the studio, and we had an optimum recording situation. George Martin has these Air Studios in Montserrat, and he's got this hot-rodded Neve that's just impossibly good. It's just the greatest recording situation, right in the middle of nowhere. You book the studio and you've got it for 24 hours a day, it's perfect.' *Lou Reed*

'*Growing Up In Public* is an album about summoning high-test courage: the courage to love and along with it the will to forgive everybody who – and everything that – ever cut short your chances in the first place . . . Reed's entire career – more accurately his entire life – has been leading up to *Growing Up In Public*. It may or may not be his finest album, but it's surely his hardest-fought victory.' *Mikal Gilmore, Rolling Stone*

'*Growing Up In Public* is one of the drinking records of all time . . . Me and Fonfara were ridiculous. We both almost drowned in the pools that they've got there. It's not a good way to make a record. We were animals.' *Lou Reed*

' "Power Of Positive Drinking" is simply written by two people who enjoy drinking.' *Lou Reed, on the song he wrote with Michael Fonfara*

'Looking back . . . for a while there I was working with musicians who were into jazz and funk. I wasn't playing guitar on my records because I really couldn't play with those guys, being a simple rock'n'roll player. I thought it would be interesting to explore that direction, but there was a gap between me and them. You can hear it on the records. So I said, "You've carried this experiment far enough. It's not working. The ideas are there and then they disappear, the music isn't consistent, you seem isolated, there's a certain confidence that's not there because you're not really in control." So I dissolved the band.' *Lou Reed*

With no further live appearances during the year, Lou appeared again only on screen – playing the part of a rock manager in Paul Simon's One Trick Pony. *It was very much a 'blink and you'll miss him' cameo role.*

'I didn't enjoy doing *One Trick Pony* at all.' *Lou Reed*

After Growing Up In Public *Lou Reed went dormant for a while. His next album, Rock And Roll Diary, was a compilation and – apart from a Christmas gig at the Bottom Line in 1980, there were no public appearances for the next year. What he did do however, was to present a series of lyrics to the glam-styled heavy metal band, Kiss – following an invitation through mutual record company connections. It seems to have been a purely financial issue as far as Reed was concerned.*

'Lou was so into our "Elder" project, that when we called and explained it over the phone to him, he said, "I'll get back to you in an hour". And he called back an hour later with good basic lyrics to "Mr Blackwell", "World Without Heroes", and a lot of other stuff that hasn't been used yet.' *Paul Stanley, Kiss*

'It's fascinating and flattering – not to mention the money – to be given a set of characters or whatever, and be asked to write songs around them.' *Lou Reed*

AFTER YEARS *of alcohol and amphetamine abuse, Lou began to busy himself with trips to Alcoholics Anonymous. He was also actively toying with several different approaches to his next album in 1981 – with the help of guitarist Robert Quine (notable for his work on Richard Hell's* Blank Generation *album), an old friend of Sylvia's.*

'I keep a notebook. I also write in my head quite a lot, or sometimes I'll write things out. It's much less a matter of doing the music first. Sometimes when that happens it comes out of a riff. And what's a good riff? Sometimes you'll get locked into one, and in the end you don't come out with a good song, just a riff.' *Lou Reed*

'About a week before going in the studio, I got together with the guitar player, and we ran down the songs together. I wrote it all out beforehand. Everyone knew the songs up to a point, but nothing was too structured.' *Lou Reed*

Returning to RCA in 1981, The Blue Mask *was finally released early the following year. Recorded at RCA's Studio C in New York, the sessions brought together Robert Quine (guitar), Fernando Saunders (bass) and Duane Perry (drums). The album was co-produced with Sean Fullan. Meanwhile, Sylvia provided the artwork for the sleeve – a clever re-working of the old* Transformer *cover.*

'This is my best album to date. This one was pretty much perfect – it came out the way it was supposed to.' *Lou Reed*

'I'm very very image conscious, and I've

Lou Reed uncorks a great one

The Blue Mask
Lou Reed
RCA
★★★★★

By Tom Carson

L OU REED'S *THE Blue Mask* is a great record, and its genius is at once so simple and unusual that the only appropriate reaction is wonder. Who expected anything like this from Reed at this late stage of the game? Even though the Velvet Underground, as critic Lester Bangs once remarked, "invented the Seventies," Reed had as much trouble as anyone else in trying to navigate the decade's actuality. By its end, he seemed to have just about removed himself from rock & roll for good. *Street Hassle*, brave and brilliant it was, had the melancholy deadly feel of a testament.

tried to use it gracefully, to focus it. On this album I'm bringing all those Lou Reeds together, into one. But the basic image is, and always has been – Lou Reed comes from New York City and writes rock'n'roll songs.' *Lou Reed*

'My goal has always been to make an album that would speak to people the way Shakespeare speaks to me, the way Joyce speaks to me – something with that kind of power, something with bite to it.' *Lou Reed*

'The intuitive responsiveness between Lou Reed and Robert Quine is a quiet summit of guitarists' interplay: the notes and noise soar

LOU MEETS THE PRESS IN 1983.

BEGINNING TO SEE THE LIGHT

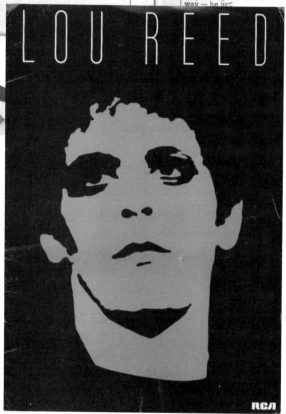

TOP: LOU REED INTERVIEWED IN *THE FACE* IN 1982. ABOVE: RCA'S PRESS PACK FOR *THE BLUE MASK*.

and dive, scudding almost formlessly until they're suddenly caught up in the focus of the rhythm . . . With *The Blue Mask*, Lou Reed has done what even John Lennon couldn't do – he's put his Plastic Ono Band and his Double Fantasy on the same record, and made us feel that, at long last, these two paths in him are joined. *Tom Carson, Rolling Stone*

Shocked by the assassination of John Lennon in December 1980, Lou definitely felt an urge to withdraw a little more from the city, and his public life there. This may be another reason for his temporary decision never to tour again – although he'd be too cool ever to admit that.

'Of course we were shocked and hurt by John Lennon's death. My parents were really worried. So we took down the "Lou Reed Lives Here" sign and moved out of New York.' *Lou Reed*

'I'm not going to tour anymore, period. It wasn't good for me. I wasn't happy with my band. Still, I did have fun. Now, I could possibly see playing New York, maybe one night at the Bottom Line. But as for 90 days and 89 cities, I can't do that anymore. I used to drink a lot. And it would be hard for me to imagine getting through one of those tours without slipping back. And I don't want to do that.' *Lou Reed*

'The songs are little plays with little characters – you hear people talking. In the song, "The Blue Mask", one person's talking to the other person and he's shouting "Take the Blue Mask off!" Or in "The Gun", the rapist turns and says, "I want you to watch your wife. I wouldn't want you to miss a second." And it's like, what? WHAT!? I have found that, without exception, any guy that listens to that song reacts with universal fear. And it's dangerous for me too. Because, like, if I do a song, and there's a bad character, or a drug character, or something like that – sometimes it's me and sometimes it's not me, but the thing is – as I sing the song, I go through it. I really do go through it. It's a really cathartic kind of thing in a lot of ways. It's interesting. It *is* acting. I always like that. But doing those characters long enough – it gets to you. Some of those lyrics are very rough.' *Lou Reed*

'My lyrics read well, I'd go as far as that. But they're certainly not poetry – the words always work far better when they're sung to a musical accompaniment.' *Lou Reed*

'I don't write for a rock'n'roll audience. I write for adults . . . who listen to rock'n'roll.' *Lou Reed*

'I'm very involved with the recording process, and the involvement's very simple. I know what I want, and how I'm gonna get it. I don't care much how we get it, actually. Technically, they develop so much every day . . . I don't want to be an engineer but I also don't want any tricks played on me. You know, engineers who throw a switch and don't tell you. All I wanted was to get the sound translated from point A to point B without losing anything. The sounds we were getting were perfect just as they were, so I didn't want any fucking around. I wanted you to listen to it as though you were sitting in a room where we were play-ing, and the way you heard it was the way it was. Each of us had worked on our instru-ments a lot getting the right tone, and we didn't need an engineer to sit around and fuck it about. See, the way I used to record

with, say, the Velvet Underground, was to go very much for the spontaneous moment. You know, write the song in the studio, do it there one time, do it to the band one time – then BAM!' *Lou Reed*

'There were no overdubs on *The Blue Mask*. Everything was done live in the studio, except the vocals.' *Lou Reed*

By way of promoting The Blue Mask, *Lou undertook a publicity tour of Europe and the States, giving press conferences in all the major cities. He also recorded an 'interview' album for the benefit of sympathetic radio stations. But there were no shows.*

THE LOU PAPERS

Steve Dupler unmasks Lou Reed

Lou Reed. What images spring to mind at the sound of the name? The darkly made-up tough boy, crowing demonically on the cover of *Rock'n'Roll Animal?* The world-weary monotone droning along behind the coloured girls on *Walk on the Wild Side?* Maybe the joyful, unleashed energy of *Metal Machine Music*, or the pure, driving Rock'n'Roll of *The Bells?*

Reed is a man of constant contrasts; an articulate and intelligent survivor in leather and dark shades – an artist who, at 40, is perhaps Rock'n'Roll's finest poet and most insightful depictor of human nature. Starting with the first album, *Velvet Underground With Nico*, released in 1967, through seventeen solo albums, Reed has played with a wildly diverse assortment of some of the finest musicians in Rock and Jazz — Steve Howe, Tony Levin, Aynsley Dunbar, Jack Bruce, the Brecker Brothers, Steve Winwood — the list goes on and on. His work with the Velvet Underground, as well as later albums like *Transformer* and *Growing Up In Public*, has shaped the framework for an entire generation of Rock'n'Rollers, some too young to even be fully aware of his influence.

After a two year hiatus, Lou Reed has returned. This time, it's with what he feels is his finest effort to date, *The Blue Mask*. Backed by an impressive and sensitive ensemble composed of Robert Quine on guitar (formerly with Richard Hell), Fernando Saunders on fretless bass (who has played live with the Mahavishnu Orchestra), Jeff Beck, and Jan Hammer), and Doane Perry (one-time drummer with the group Rivits), Reed has created an emotional conceptual album, characterised by its total spontaneity and lack of overdubs and studio sleight-of-hand.

Our meeting takes place in the opulent East Side Manhattan town house/office of his manager. Surprisingly, Reed does not look out of place in the plush meeting room. He is instead relaxed and at ease with himself, though it was not always so. He has turned out a killer of a record with *The Blue Mask*, and he knows it. No question about that.

IM&RW: Do you cringe when you hear yourself referred to as the "Father of New W

L.R.: No, no. I c

IM&RW: Ho

L.R.: I'd lik

IM&RW: And th   s   e was actually just a straigh   um, right? I   ply one overdub?   st one overdub, and it's a great one. On the end of *My House*. It's a chord solo with my special guitar.

IM&RW: Oh, yeah. That's sort of a bridge between *My House* and *Women*.

L.R.: Right. And it's such a trick, you know? Every time I listen to it, I only listen for one thing — that's when the power guitar makes its first entrance. I had to make sure it wasn't too loud, too ominous sounding. It had to just be BIG, but happy sounding. Just placing that in the right place — well, it had to be just right. Of course, it was *my* decision. I've listened to it since. A lot. It's in the right place.

IM&RW: This isn't the first time you've done an album in this format, is it? No overdubbing, I mean.

L.R.: Oh, sure. The Velvet Underground albums didn't have a lot o' overdubs. Maybe one or two little things, here and there. Some of my own albums, like *The Bells*, didn't have a lot of overdubbing either. But this one in particular is approached with all the same ideas as before, except this time I wrote it all out beforehand. Everybody knew the songs up to a point, but nothing was *too* structured.

IM&RW: How did you go about selecting the band members for The Blue Mask? You've not played with any of them before.

L.R.: Well, I wasn't going to use that band I'd hung around my neck for so long. I went out looking, but I was open to suggestion. The drummer (Doane Perry), I'd played with once before.

IM&RW: Is he British?

L.R.: No. He's from New York. I don' think much of English guitar players, and all that. Or English Rock'n'Roll groups, fo' *h''   '''   '''*'t. Not th thin' An +'

cents. You know, give me the money, thanks. (laughs) I think it's great.

IM&RW: Let's talk about The Blue Mask. Why are you calling this your best album to date? Can you   obl '''   hout it?
                           m a pretty
                           Te'

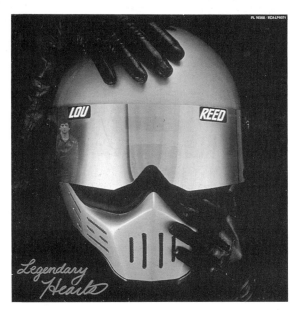

PL 14568 / RCA LP6071

'I've always liked those very basic, very simple rock and roll changes. I've never heard anything I like more than that. Not in opera, not in classical music, not in jazz, nor in show tunes. Nothing. Nothing has impressed me as much as the most basic rock'n'roll chord change, and by that I mean, say, E to A. And to this day, when I hear the change done right – and it can be

done wrong – I get an abnormal degree of pleasure from it. Wouldn't it be wonderful to put a melody over that, something that would stick like grease? And then wouldn't it be great if the lyrics also had some substance to them, were as simple and as elegant as that change from one chord to another?' *Lou Reed*

'It's very hard to keep it simple.' *Lou Reed*

Legendary Hearts was recorded at the tail end of 1982 with the help of Robert Quine (guitar), Fernando Saunders (bass) and Fred Maher (drums) – the album marking Lou's eventual and inevitable return to live work. To kick off, he played a show at the Bottom Line, in front of an audience that included Andy Warhol. The show was filmed, and released on video as A Night With Lou Reed.

'I always like my most recent album best, and that applies to every single one of them. I'm always excited about the last one when I get out of the studio, and then having heard it so much, I'll suddenly get very sick of it and won't listen to it for a year or so. I always find that I don't discover what the songs are really about until maybe a year later.' *Lou Reed*

LOU REED
THE LOU REED COMMENTARIES BY CHRIS BOHN
ON THE MILD SID
PHOTOGRAPHY»ANTON CORBIJN

From Underground Monster to Metal Machine Heart — the new homeloving Lou comes in off the street and lays his legend to rest

lou reed

live in italy

Pic Anton Corbijn

GHOSTS
IN THE METAL MACHINE

LOU REED
Live In Italy *(RCA)*

GROWING UP in public (a further instalment).
Lou's going on 42, and 'Live In Italy' documents how he regards his history as of September 1983, just as 'Take No Prisoners' did in '79, 'Rock 'n' Roll Animal' and 'Lou Reed Live' five years previously, and, of course, '1969 The Velvet Underground Live' five years before *that*.
And when I say history I mean that seven out of 15 tracks are The Velvet

recently been at such pains to stress his new-found peace and inspiration through domestic bliss?
Perhaps by daring to reinterpret the looming vignettes and confessionals of old in the laconic, even laid back, voice of *now*, he demonstrates that they are *only* songs, *his* songs he can tame and twist at will.
And maybe secondly, as Lou sung back in '76, *"deep down inside I got a rock and roll heart"*. He told Chris Bohn last year that "Nothing has impressed me as much

playing 'Heroin'
mean Lou hank
poetic spring of
lost *innocence?*
Or . . . becaus
Quine, Lou Reed
found another s
guitarist, and he
delighted to spa
'Sister Ray' and
great old songs
frustratingly, jus
played right for i
Lou and the ex
in an empathetic
glass grid, an alu
which spirals int
lyrical solos, eve
as on a stunning
Sons'; Verlaine a
spring to mind. A
Television, rhyth
and slightly jazzy
drumming is a lit
and lumpy, but F
Saunders' quirki
fretless bass boo
buoyantly thoug
pathos when nee
The trebley, Fe
this clipped and
bears the same re
today's post-Noc
rock as did the 'R
Animal' band's tc
glam-power chor
Now, anxiety is th
neurotic tension
present but
erupting
su

'Lou's lyrics you can understand now, and the music was really loud. He did a lot of familiar songs, but you didn't recognise them, they sounded different.' *Andy Warhol*

September 1983 saw Lou and his band visiting Italy, where he had maintained enormous popularity over the years. Some of the shows were recorded and released early in 1984 as an album entitled Live In Italy. *Increasingly interested in making soundtrack contributions, Lou made a couple of donations to an animated movie* Rock And Rule *(released in 1983), following it up with a song ('Hot Hips') for the John Travolta/Jamie Lee Curtis film,* Perfect.

In order to provide himself with a higher profile in the mid-eighties, Lou took a deliberately commercial approach to the recording of his next album, New Sensations. *The resulting single, 'I Love You Suzanne', became his biggest hit in years.*

'Just because I write about what I write about, doesn't mean I don't care about what's going on around me. The days of me being aloof about certain things are over.' *Lou Reed*

'I wanted to have fun with *New Sensations.*

There were certain sounds I heard on the radio – a certain kind of bass drum for instance – that were really strong and exciting, and I wanted to have that. I've spent a lot of time recently getting into the tone of the guitar.' *Lou Reed*

LOU REED NEW SENSATIONS

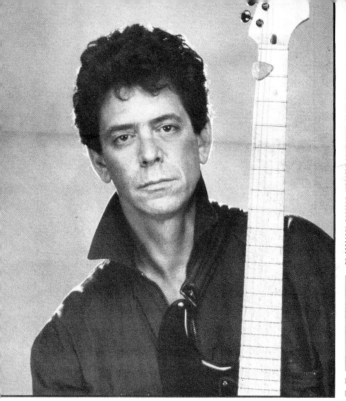

Some talk tough and some talk dirty but the new LOU REED won't talk at all.
KRISTINE McKENNA finds it's a case of less lurid more loured at.

'I refuse to get involved in the argument of "are videos good or bad for music?" That doesn't remotely interest me. Video is here to stay. It can bring music to the attention of people who might not be exposed to it otherwise. Personally – and I can only speak for myself, I can't speak for other people – I see video as an ad for the album and that's how I approach it.' *Lou Reed*

New Sensations *sold better than anything he'd done in ten years, so to capitalise, Lou reversed his earlier ban and embarked on a massive tour of America, Europe and Australia in 1984. Keen to take advantage of any further easy pickings, he also accepted an offer to help promote Honda Scooters.*

'We're going to take a walk on the wild side, to portray the spirit of adventure and excitement involved with scootering . . . Reed is an innovator, one of the pioneers of new music. His music is unique and experimental – much like scooters.' *Neil Leventhal, Honda's Motor Scooter Manager*

'Who else could make a scooter hip?' *Lou Reed*

LOU GIVES A MONOSYLLABIC AND SOMETIMES HOSTILE INTERVIEW TO THE NEW MUSICAL EXPRESS IN LONDON.

With the inevitable cries of 'sell-out' ringing in his ears, Lou defended his subsequent decision to advertise American Express cards by pointing an accusing finger at the naivety of his critics.

'Look who's recording you – the same companies who manufacture missiles. You could really start tearing it apart.' *Lou Reed*

'I do commercials for money and to try to sell my records. The main thing is to get people to listen to the records, because I really like them, and I think that people would really like them. Plus, if you get into one of my records, there's like 17 or 18 records sitting back there. I'm not a bad thing to get addicted to.' *Lou Reed*

'What I see myself as is a writer. Whether I'm a nice guy, whether I'm a liar, whether I'm immoral, should have nothing to do with it.' *Lou Reed*

In 1985 Polydor released a compilation of outtakes from the Velvet Underground's MGM ses-

Don't settle for walking.

HONDA

sions of 1969. The album, VU, *led to a massive resurgence of interest in the band. The following year a second archive release,* Another View, *led to a special profile on the band being commissioned by London Weekend Television, for inclusion in their* South Bank Show *series. Only Lou kept his distance during this 'reunion' while, curiously perhaps, Andy Warhol appeared not to have been invited.*

'John Cale says that the Velvets broke up before we accomplished what we should have accomplished. I think he's right in a way. My records are my version of it. John's records are his version of it. The drumming of Maureen Tucker is something that can't be replaced by anyone. And then of course, *Loaded* didn't have Maureen on it, and that's a lot of people's favourite Velvet Underground record, so we can't get too lost in the mystique of it all.' *Lou Reed*

'The Velvet Underground would have loved to have been popular.' *Lou Reed*

'I mean, I just don't understand why I have never gotten a penny from that first Velvet Underground record. That record really sells, and I was the producer! Shouldn't I get something? I mean, shouldn't I? . . . What I can't figure out, is when Lou stopped liking me. I mean, he even went out and got himself two dachshunds like I had, and then after that he started not liking me, but I don't know exactly why or when. Maybe it was when he married this last wife, maybe he decided that he didn't want to see peculiar people.' *Andy Warhol*

'We actually had a rule in the Velvets for a while – if anybody played a blues lick, they'd be fined. Of course we didn't have any money to fine anybody with, but that was because there were so many of these blues bands around all copping on that. And while

I really like the stuff for singing, I can't sing that. I had to find my own way.' *Lou Reed*

'The VU albums, like my own, are implicitly about freedom of expression – freedom to write about what you please in any way you please.' *Lou Reed*

In the Autumn of 1985, Lou joined up with rock and country stars like Willie Nelson and Neil Young, to play the Farm Aid charity show in the States. This was a domestic fund-raiser inspired by Bob Dylan's remarks during that summer's Live Aid event. Dylan had requested that some of the money collected for the Ethiopean appeal should be redirected to the bank accounts of hard-up and over-taxed US farmers. Typically antagonistic, the new cause did attract a lot of support however, including Reed's. The New Yorker then followed up by lending similar support for the Artists United Against Apartheid project, spearheaded by Stevie Van Zandt.

'I couldn't not be vocal about apartheid.' *Lou Reed*

The next album, Mistrial, *was released in the summer of 1986, to little effect. His final cut for RCA, it was co-produced earlier that year with Fernando Saunders, who also played bass and rhythm guitar. Other musicians included J.P Lewis (drums) and Sammy Merendino (drum programming).*

'I've had the best reviews in the world and the worst ones. I've had reviews that say, "Why don't you just die?" and it hasn't seemed to make any difference.' *Lou Reed*

'A lot of times, what fan letters say is illuminating to me, because they take something in a way that I literally wasn't aware of. I'm not the expert on my own work. I'm not being cute when I say I don't really know what the album's about. Give me two or three years distance on it, then I'll start figuring out just what's in those lyrics.' *Lou Reed*

' "The Original Wrapper" was designed to be the all-time rap lyric. I read it to my friend Jim Carroll and he said, "You already did that with *Street Hassle*," and I said, "Oh, that's true".' *Lou Reed*

'I kept thinking about writing the great American novel. I think my novel is all these things lined up and played in order. It's very easy to see that the person who wrote the Velvet Underground stuff wrote *Mistrial*. It's not all that different, it's just a little older.' *Lou Reed*

What gained him more prestige than the release of Mistrial *however, was his involvement with that summer's Amnesty International benefit tour. Joining forces with the likes of U2, Peter Gabriel, Tracey Chapman, Sting, Brian Adams and others, Lou played a series of stadium shows across Europe and America. He also appeared at the more low-key* Secret Policeman's Third Ball *in London (also in aid of Amnesty), where he performed a specially composed number, 'Voices Of Freedom'.*

'It was just great to be involved.' *Lou Reed*

With no 'hit' potential on his latest album, Lou scored his biggest chart success since 1973 with a curious performance of Sam and Dave's classic 'Soul Man' – from an obscure film of the same name, released in 1986, starring C. Thomas Howell. Much to Warhol's displeasure however (Warhol had his own video company at this time), Lou chose someone else to make the video. This seems to have enhanced the rift between the two men.

'Lou Reed sat in my row at the MTV awards, but never looked over. I don't understand Lou. Why doesn't he talk to me now?' *Andy Warhol, from his diaries*

Following a routine gallbladder operation at the New York Hospital, Andy Warhol died on 22 February 1987. When the artist's diaries were published, Reed's sense of guilt was compounded.

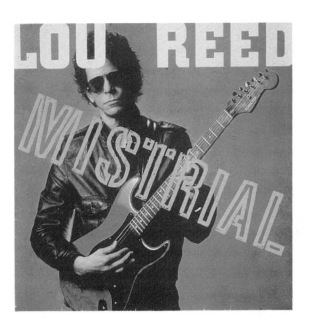

THE SLEEVE OF *MISTRIAL*, LOU REED'S FINAL ALBUM FOR RCA.

'I hate Lou Reed more and more, I really do, because he's not giving us any video work.' *Andy Warhol, the last mention of Lou in his diaries*

'Andy and I had had a very major falling out. Em, I was in touch, but not close. Because Andy's always tape-recording everything. And I didn't want anything to be tape-recorded. I'm not one of those people, I wasn't that way in the Factory and I'm still not one. There were some things that for personal kinds of reasons, I kept him at a discreet arm's length.' *Lou Reed*

'Andy had a great effect on my formative years. I like and admire him very much.' *Lou Reed, typically referring to the late artist in the present tense*

'Andy's way of looking at things, I miss. I owe him that. His whole aesthetic. I still wonder, if I look at something new and interesting, oh, I wonder how Andy'd think about that? Not having him about to contribute this totally unique way of looking at things, I miss that a lot.' *Lou Reed*

123

BY THE *beginning of 1987 Lou was working with the Latin American salsa star, Ruben Blades, on the latter's album* Nothing But The Truth. *Since they were old friends, it made an ideal working holiday for Lou. He also recorded a song ('Something Happened') for the Keanu Reeves film* Permanent Record *(Lou even made an appearance, as a rock star), and went in search of a new recording contract – ending up at WEA's Sire label.*

'I don't know why people give me record deals. I think it's because they at least break even, and I think they even make a few bucks while they're at it. I'm a cult figure, but I sell some records.' *Lou Reed*

It would be another two years however, before the release of Lou's next album, New York *– assisted in its creation by a young guitar protégé from Boston, Mike Rathke, who was yet another friend of Sylvia's.*

'I can't do anything outside of New York. It's death.' *Lou Reed*

'Freedom, endless opportunities in everything – films, Chinese culture, people, places, things – a city of wonderful, impossible mixtures and energies. The only city in the world deserving the name. What I don't like – crime, traffic, a criminal subway system, a city government that is oblivious to the plight and feelings of the poor, the minorities, the homeless . . . Antiquated criminal justice system, antiquated civil service and union rules, regulations and membership, second-rate public school system.' *Lou Reed, in his contribution to* New York *magazine, on what he likes about New York*

'I'm pretty upset about what's going on in New York City after eight years of Reagan. This government's been picking on all the people who can't defend themselves, and it's passed so far into the surreal now that you can't even satirise it.' *Lou Reed*

'Since the whole Reagan years thing, things moved so far to the right so fast that, y'know, the good guys are still sittin' round having philosophical debates, while the others just get tighter. But it's hard to believe that film-makers and writers and rock'n'rollers haven't been tackling this stuff. I don't get it. Creative people just aren't responding, really.' *Lou Reed*

'I see it every day, things going backwards – the system not working. You got disease and drugs and the whole hardening of public attitudes towards Aids. Y'know, the fundamentalist line that if you get it, you deserve it. These guys are on the level of African witchdoctors, they wanna reverse progress. Why do people wanna go back? It's painful, all this negativism. The blueprint for chaos . . . Whatever you see as an outsider, I'm here to tell you that it's worse than that.' *Lou Reed*

'I'm for legalisation of drugs. All this prohibition stuff – think what you could do with all the money they spend trying to right drugs. Legalise it . . . Tax it, make it pure, stop the disease, the killing, the crime. I mean, they can't stop it 'cos the market for it is so gigantic. That's the bottom line. We're tied to all these markets in the first place, all these other countries. But, like, if they took the huge illegal profit out of it,

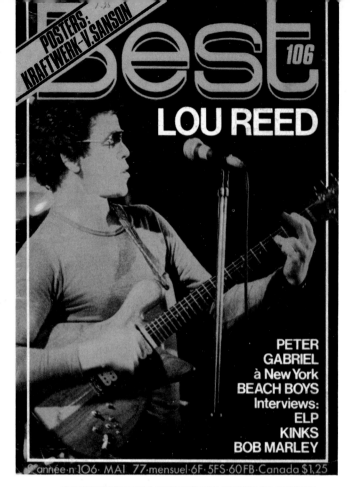

best 106

LOU REED

PETER
GABRIEL
à New York
BEACH BOYS
Interviews:
ELP
KINKS
BOB MARLEY

année·n 106· MAI 77·mensuel·6F·5FS·60FB·Canada $1,25

LOU REED'S POPULARITY NEVER WANED IN FRANCE.

that'd hurt them. Imagine it – big deal, there's a drug store. It'd be cheap too. OK, some drugs, I personally think, you should only be able to get when you're over 50. If you live past 50, you can try Ecstacy or whatever the hell you want. But legalise the shit, take the taboo and glamour out of it.' *Lou Reed*

'New York is like this huge person that's shaped me as much as genetics.' *Lou Reed*

Recorded and mixed at New York's Media Sound studios during the second half of 1988, the New York *album was finally released in January 1989. Lou co-produced the album with Fred Maher, who also played drums on most of the tracks. The other drummer was Mo Tucker, who contributed to a couple of numbers –* Last Great American Whale *and* Dimestore Mystery. *Mike Rathke (guitar) and Rob Wasserman (bass) augmented the line-up.*

'*New York* is my first real record for years. I had a lot of time to think about what I wanted to say. I re-wrote every song six or seven times to get them focussed, and got all the guitar sounds on top of them that I really like. This is the absolute first time an album has actually come out the way I heard it in my head. I've objected to a lot of things in my time, but these days I'm doing something about it.' *Lou Reed*

'It's interesting from a writing point of view, the techniques I used, the sequence is

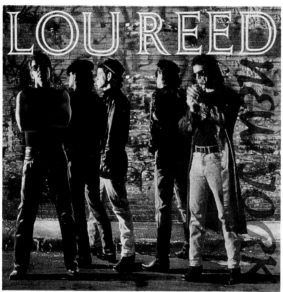

NEW YORK HAD ALWAYS BEEN THE INSPIRATION FOR LOU REED'S WORK. IT WAS INEVITABLE THAT HE WOULD EVENTUALLY PRODUCE AN ALBUM ABOUT IT.

important. Because every time you're hit with a song, you've been hit with a few others before it. There have been these other things whispered in your ear, setting you up for what that song's going to talk about. In "Romeo Had Juliet" you have the two teens. You have "Halloween Parade", people dying of Aids. Then Pedro in the welfare hotel in "Dirty Blvd". Then you have these two people who are fighting ("Endless Cycle"), and what if they have a kid? Then it's into the ecology, "Last Great American Whale" – and suddenly you've got a guy talking about

"Gee, maybe I ought to have a kid" – the beginning of "The Great Adventure". But while he's been talking about that, you've been loaded up with five other ones. What has been happening to the kids, what is happening to the land? I've been privately talking about these things with a lot of people, about what is really going on. And as a writer that really drew my attention. It's perfectly possible that maybe I'll put out a party record next. But in my own way, I think this is a party record, just not the kind you're used to.' *Lou Reed*

'See, what *New York* is about, what it is actually about, over and above the stuff I'm singing about, is the use of language. People haven't really picked that up.' *Lou Reed*

'Jeez, what a great title. Give me a good title and I'm home free. I wrote the first version and it was horrible, but I'm not interested in whether it's good or bad, I just want the thing written out. Then I will go someplace with it.' *Lou Reed, on the creation of 'The Last Great American Whale'*

'I did what I always do, the only change has been – and I know it sounds cliched – but if you practise something over and over and over, you're supposed to get better at it.' *Lou Reed*

'I've become completely well adjusted to being a cult figure.' *Lou Reed*

'The fourteen songs on *New York* – which runs nearly an hour – are fierce poetic journalism, a reportage of surreal horror in which the unyielding force of actual circum-stances continually threatens to overwhelm the ordering power of art. Reed, of course, is no stranger to unhinging scenes of squalor. On his inestimably influential early albums with the Velvet Underground, and through much of his solo work in the seven-ties, Reed cast a cold eye on virtually every manner of human excess. But times have changed, and Reed's attitudes have changed with them. A walk on the sexually undiffer-entiated wild side is no longer simply an outrageous means of spitting in the face of the bourgeoisie, but a potentially fatal journey.' *Anthony De Curtis, Rolling Stone*

'If Bob Dylan was plugged into the eighties the way he once was to the sixties, perhaps he could have come up with a commentary on the times to match this. Right now it is hard to think of anyone else who has come close.' *David Sinclair, The Times*

'I always go out and get the latest Dylan album. Bob Dylan can turn a phrase man. Like the album *Down In The Groove*, his choice of songs. "Going Ninety Miles An Hour Down A Dead End Street" – I'd give anything if I could have written that. Or that other one – "Rank Strangers To Me". The key word there is "Rank".' *Lou Reed*

'I don't even own an acoustic guitar. I know I should, it'd be a lot simpler but, from day one, it's always been electric. It affects the way you play, the way you think.' *Lou Reed*

'Some people really like having the spotlight on them, I don't. What I like is the song, and performing it. Doing it for people who like it. I want out of the rock'n'roll thing, I really do. It's a little late now, but I don't enjoy that end of it. Yet there I am, up on stage, performing my stuff. Certainly part of the reason, originally, is that no-one else would. And I still think, to some extent, I do me really well.' *Lou Reed*

'For a while, I felt a little self-compelled to write Lou Reed type of songs. I should have understood that a Lou Reed song was anything that I wanted to write about.' *Lou Reed*

'It's interesting when you've been around as long as I have, to see these things come around. It's like, do you wanna be serious

**GROWING OLD GRACEFULLY: LOU REED CULTIVATES
THE SERIOUS ACADEMIC LOOK IN THE LATER 1980s.**

about your own life? And if you don't wanna be serious, there's party records – and that's a lot of fun. But I'm interested in something else. I'm not saying it's better than all the rest, it's just different. I have a few more words at my disposal, and I can't ignore that.' *Lou Reed*

Just prior to the completion of the New York *album, the Velvet Underground camp was struck by another tragedy – the death of Nico. While cycling in Europe she fell, hit her head and died of a cerebral haemorrhage. In the years since her departure from the Velvet Underground, Nico had pursued an erratic solo career, periodically releasing albums of limited appeal. Basing herself in Britain for much of the time, she'd got involved in the Punk scene of the late seventies, and developed a relationship with Punk poet John Cooper Clark. At the time of Nico's death, John Cale was already busy on an instrumental tribute to Warhol, and having invited Reed to listen to the tapes, this latest tragedy seemed to add momentum to the project. The result would be* Songs For Drella.

NICO AND ANDY WARHOL IN NEW YORK IN THE MID-1980s. WARHOL'S DEATH IN 1986 WAS FOLLOWED TRAGICALLY THREE YEARS LATER BY NICO'S DEATH AS A RESULT OF A CYCLING ACCIDENT.

'John [Cale] and I just rented out a small rehearsal studio for three weeks, and locked ourselves in.' *Lou Reed*

'It began as just the two of us throwing ideas around, but gradually it turned into song-writing . . . I was really excited by the amount of power just two people could do without needing drums, because what we have there is such a strong core idea that the simpler the better . . . Although I think [Lou] did most of the work, he has allowed me to keep a position of dignity in the process.' *John Cale*

In January 1989 Reed and Cale performed Songs For Drella *in front of an audience at St Ann's Church, Brooklyn – even though the material was not yet complete.* New York *was ready for release however, and in March Lou set*

129

off on American and European tours to promote the work. Meanwhile an out-take from the New York *sessions, 'The Room', was included on the UK release of the single 'Dirty Blvd'.*

'They kept saying, "Don't you have anything you left off"? Why should somebody buy the single if they've already got the album? I said, "When they put *Moby Dick* out do you think they said – in the paperback version let's leave out chapter 13." Anyway, I didn't have anything. Then I said, "I remember one little jam Mike and I did that was great fun. Maybe I can find it on cassette." *Lou Reed*

August saw yet another US tour, with Mo Tucker providing the support. The trip was soon curtailed however, after Lou broke his ankle falling down a staircase. He was able to keep in the public eye though, by making guest appearances on new albums by Simple Minds and Dion. Also, after further reworkings with John Cale, Songs For Drella *was ready for its premiere at the Brooklyn Academy of Music on 30 November 1989. The album was finally released in May 1990*

'The thing I was disturbed about with *Drella*, was these evil books presenting Andy Warhol as just a piece of fluff. I wanted to show the Andy I knew. I wouldn't call it working through emotions. There's a craft to all this – it's not just spewing out emotions. It's very ordered and very specific work.' *Lou Reed*

'I don't go to clubs, I don't go to concerts. See, after being with Andy [Warhol], if I never went to another one of those things it would be too soon. And I still feel that way. I get cards from all these places, but l don't go. Not interested. I'm kinda dull, huh?' *Lou Reed*

'I'm into this for the long haul. I feel I've just started to get a grip on it, what I can do with it, what I want to do with it, and who I'd like to take with me when I do it. It's really easy in a sense, because the people who like it will go with me, and the people who don't will say I'm full of shit, and more power to them. They don't want me, and I'm not interested in them either. That's OK. I have no problem with that.' *Lou Reed*

Perhaps more widely admired now than at any time during his career, Lou was happy to lend his celebrity status to a whole string of worthy causes. Following an appearance at the Nelson Mandela concert at Wembley Stadium, London in April 1990 (Lou performed 'Dirty Blvd' and 'Last Great American Whale') he went to Prague to give support to Vaclav Havel the once-persecuted playwright who was now president of the recently democratised Czechoslovakia. He was also assigned to interview Havel for Rolling Stone *magazine. The publication never printed it.*

'I'm a genuinely nice guy, I really am. But I think I'm temperamental, and I'm talking about me, today. I think I have a pretty good handle on it. But sometimes temperamental can be misconstrued as being difficult. I've certainly been really difficult in the past, but that's because I was beset, and I didn't have it together. It's a different story now, of course, I'm older. Supposedly when you get older you get something from all of it before – or you drop dead and that's the end of it. I think I know about certain things better than other people, and I'll fight for it. And I don't think that's being difficult, I mean, it sounds tacky, but it's like being true to your vision.' *Lou Reed*

On 15 June l990, Lou Reed and John Cale were booked to play at the opening of the 'Andy Warhol Exposition' at the Cartier Foundation in France – an event which also included a spectacular multi-media homage to the Velvet Underground. At the end of the set Sterling Morrison and Maureen Tucker joined them on stage for a frenetic rendition of Heroin.

Later that year Reed and Cale travelled to Japan to perform Songs For Drella. *In December, Reed lined up alongside Kylie Minogue and Wet Wet Wet at the John Lennon tribute concert (the tenth anniversary of his death) in Liverpool. Lou played two of Lennon's songs, 'Jealous Guy' and 'Mother'.*

News Special: Your favourite band is BROKE! ★ **UB40**
GO-BETWEENS ★ **KAZUKO's KARAOKE**

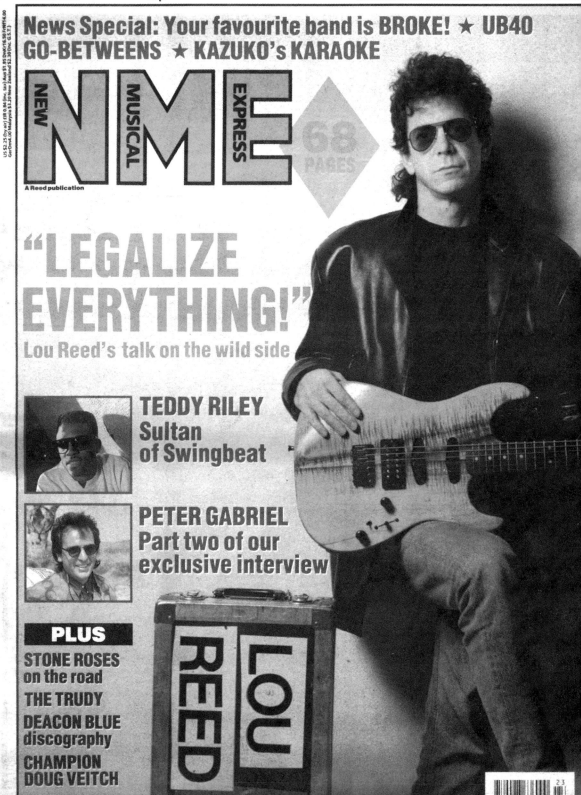

NME
NEW MUSICAL EXPRESS
A Reed publication

68 PAGES

"LEGALIZE EVERYTHING!"
Lou Reed's talk on the wild side

TEDDY RILEY
Sultan of Swingbeat

PETER GABRIEL
Part two of our exclusive interview

PLUS
STONE ROSES
on the road
THE TRUDY
DEACON BLUE
discography
CHAMPION DOUG VEITCH

US $2.25 (by air) EIR 0.84 (inc. tax) Aus $1.95 (inc)(16.50)HMT14.00 GerDm4.00 Malaysia $3.20 New Zealand $2.30 (inc. G.S.T.)

9 770028 636000

9. The Power and the Glory

EARLY 1991 saw Lou in New York's Magic Shop studio, working on the album Magic And Loss. *Co-producing the work with guitarist Mike Rathke, other musicians included Rob Wasserman (bass) and Michael Blair (drums). As in recent years, the technical approach was of particular importance, and Lou actually spent longer mixing the album than he did recording it. After much attention to detail the album was finally ready for release in January 1992. At the same time an anthology of Reed's lyrics,* Between Thought And Expression, *was published – while European and American tours were set up to promote the two.*

'I made all my mistakes in public and on record to boot, so you know I have made life very difficult for myself. People think I'm being falsely modest when I say I believe records are collaborative, just the way films are, but I'm only really as good as the people I'm working with. And it's not easy to find them. I've got years and years to prove that. I'm not one of these wunderkinds who goes in and plays all the instruments himself, I'm just the guitar player and the writer. I've had a lot of problems – and I mean a lot, coming to grips with how to use studios. Just reading the directions of those machines is difficult. And then there's how to control the engineer.' *Lou Reed*

'This record sounds good on a beatbox. I wanted people to be able to walk round the sound, to be able to picture the people playing it and, locate them, even pick out different instruments if you want. But also, on expensive equipment, you should be able to get deeper and deeper into it. For the longest time, the only place I could hear my stuff like that was through friends in hi-fi stores who have those rooms out the back with equipment so expensive you can't even imagine who buys it. The secret is consistency. I've got to be able to hear it wherever I'm listening.' *Lou Reed*

'Maybe to relate to this album you need to have been whacked around by life a bit. This record won't mean that much to an eight-year-old, except that the sound is really fun. You can just luxuriate in the sound, it's so thick, defined and dimensional.' *Lou Reed*

Dealing as it did with the subject of death, the album was widely considered to be rather gloomy.

'Magic and Loss is Lou Reed's most affecting, emotionally direct solo work since *The Blue Mask*, a stunning consummation of that

WALK ON THE MILD SIDE

While his Sixties contemporaries sold out, cleaned up or died, the singer and songwriter Lou Reed long hung on to the rock and roll essentials: drugs, sunglasses worn indoors, and a famously bad temper. Now, reports GILES SMITH, there are some signs of a new, softer, edge to New York's archetypal rock hero. Photograph by ROBIN BARTON

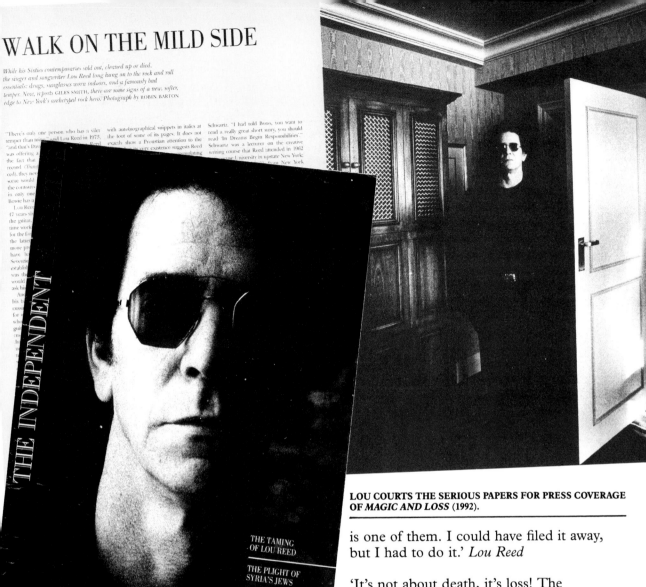

'There's only one person who has a viler temper than mine,' said Lou Reed in 1973, 'and that's Dav... Reed was offering a... fact that *Trans...* cord), they nev... some would... the contours... in only one... Bowie has sa...

Lou Ree... 47 years si... the guitar... time work... for the fo... the latter... more pr... have be... Seventi... establish... was the... would... ask hi...

An... his h... consis... for w... gui... cup... ha... s...

with autobiographical snippets in italics at the foot of some of its pages. It does not exactly show a Proustian attention to the ... its very existence suggests Reed...

Schwartz. "I had told Bono, you want to read a really great short story, you should read 'In Dreams Begin Responsibilities'." Schwartz was a lecturer on the creative writing course that Reed attended in 1962 ... rse University in upstate New York; ... from New York...

THE TAMING OF LOU REED

THE PLIGHT OF SYRIA'S JEWS

THE MYSTERY OF A VANISHING CON MAN

IS AMERICA DOOMED?

14 DECEMBER 1991

LOU COURTS THE SERIOUS PAPERS FOR PRESS COVERAGE OF *MAGIC AND LOSS* (1992).

---

album's naked guitar clamour, the hushed chapel intimacy of the third Velvet Underground album and the barbed reportorial vitality of Reed's best songwriting. He offers no great moral revelations and no happy ever after, just big questions and some basic horse sense. "There's a bit of magic in everything," he sings, at the very end of the record, "and then some loss to even things out."' *David Fricke, Rolling Stone*

'I did have doubts. But as a writer there's only a couple of really big themes, and death

is one of them. I could have filed it away, but I had to do it.' *Lou Reed*

'It's not about death, it's loss! The rock'n'roll record is considered a tinker toy medium because no-one is writing about it on that level. I want to move the thing, to make it something that can help people in their lives. This sounds pretentious, but I mean it. I'm not kidding around.' *Lou Reed*

'This isn't a bleak record. I'm not the only person in the world who's experienced loss – especially these days with what Aids and other diseases are doing. These are complex emotions . . . The record is like a friend talking to you. It's cleansing for the soul. That's why I think it's such a positive record because it gives you something you can really grasp onto. This record gives the listener something more than music. When loss enters your life, what do you do? Do you go out and get drunk? In the end you wake up, the person's still gone. You can't stay drunk forever – you've still got to deal with it.' *Lou Reed*

'I wouldn't call *Magic And Loss* grieving. I think of this as a gift to listeners, it's a life lesson about how you deal with loss. Of course, it helps if the listener has a little life experience – it's not aimed at little girls. These people that died, there's so much to be learned from them. I think of this as a very up record, because it's how you get something positive out of something so seemingly tragic as that. And yet in this particular situation, there's a magic that transforms things. The magic is what makes it possible to deal with something like this.' *Lou Reed*

'It's a celebration of friendship and transcendence. The singer goes through all the conflicting emotions associated with death, like, "Why didn't I call on you last Thursday? Why didn't I say goodbye? Why did I go to the store instead?"' *Lou Reed*

'One of the people this record is about is Doc Pomus, a great friend of mine. Not a day goes by when I'm not painfully aware that I can't just pick up the phone and call him and hear his growling voice. The other person's name is Rita . . .' *Lou Reed*

'I really loved Doc. He was an amazing creature, though I only got to know him in the last coupla years. A mutual friend said we should meet and I only lived two blocks away from him, so I started traipsing round. I went to his Writers' Workshop, and it was

SOMBRE

Lou Reed: death and how to deal with it.

LOU REED
Magic & Loss
SIRE WX 435

Since powering his way back into everybody's good books three years ago with the New York album, Lou Reed has become more creatively focused than at any point in his 25-year career. His current pre-occupation – death and how to deal with it – first surfaced on the Songs For 'Drella tribute to Andy Warhol, performed with fellow Velvet John Cale. But that was a party album compared to the sombre deliberations of Magic And Loss: an unflinchingly detailed response to the (natural) deaths in 1990 of two of his friends, Doc Pomus and a woman called Rita, which traces Reed's grim progress from the cancer ward to the crematorium.

The song titles – Sword Of Damocles, Goodbye Mass, Cremation, Gassed and Stoked – tell it like it horribly is: the awful reality of radiation therapy, isotopes in lungs, hard chairs in the chapel of rest and phone lines being permanently disconnected has been minutely and vividly logged. Nor is there a happy ending. The album concludes with the obscure and only faintly comforting suggestion of the title track – something about how the experience of loss can be purgative,

KEN SHARP

a real thrill for these people to have their songs edited by him. I just went over to talk, but not as much as I wished.' *Lou Reed*

'It has a beginning, middle and end . There's a song, "The Power And The Glory" – that's repeated, but the song is transformed when it is repeated. At the beginning of the record, the song is defining the situation and the illness from the outside – you loved the life that others throw away nightly. Towards the end of the record, the song reappears, but this time it's upbeat, not melancholy, and it's approached proudly. The album is about how that transformation takes place.' *Lou Reed*

'The character singing "Warrior King – Revenge" is very mad at the elements that have attacked and killed his friends. But it's not aimed at a person. It's aimed at a thing. There's no person to take it out on with terminal illness. It's not like you can take it in an alley and do this, this, and this. If I could. . . but with death you can't.' *Lou Reed*

'There's also a line in "Magician" that goes, "My hand can't hold a cup of coffee". I remember, to hold a cup of coffee, they had to put gloves on their hands because the chemotherapy affects them so badly. The glove is to give the hand form. I didn't want to relay that image. It was enough to know that your hand couldn't hold a cup of coffee, and let it go at that . . . But it was hard to sing knowing that. I called up that vision every time I did it. And imagine the kind of restraint I'm talking about, to just sing "My hand can't hold a cup of coffee" and leave it at that, when I knew there was so much more there. I know what I'm talking about here, it's all accurate. I'm not making any of it up. I was the kind of person who would check up on the doctors treating my friends.' *Lou Reed*

'In many ways, this was easier than anything I've ever done. It was clear, it was focused. I knew what I wanted out of it, and I knew how to go and get it. That part was not hard.' *Lou Reed*

'How do you deal with illness in a society that doesn't talk about it. They certainly don't talk about it in rock'n'roll, not in the way they write about it in novels, in stage plays. Even in a rotten movie from Hollywood like *Love Story*. But you don't have anything of any depth in rock.' *Lou Reed*

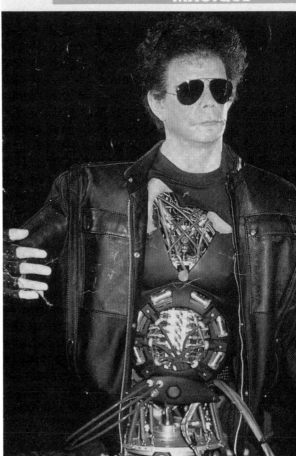

Arrêt sur image

MAGIQUE

Newlook hurle avec le Lou

Lou Reed, rocker quinquagé-naire et impudent, s'en est

intensité que la rédaction de faili partir dere de spleen au C Thanks Lou, il n

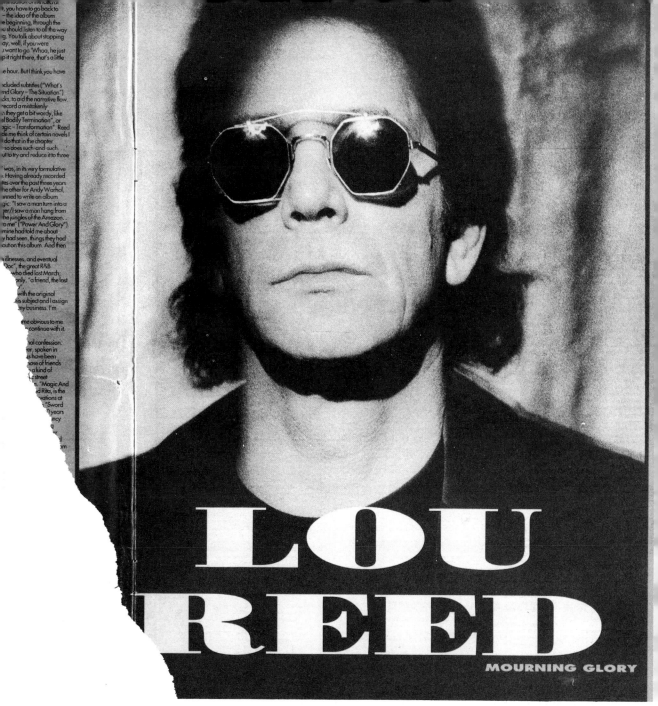

you have to go back to
– the idea of the album
beginning, through the
u should listen to all the way
g. You talk about stopping
ay, well, if you were
want to go 'Whoa, he just
p it right there, that's a little

e hour. But I think you have

cluded subtitles ("What's
nd Glory – The Situation")
cks, to aid the narrative flow.
n they get a bit wordy, like
Bodily Termination", or
gic – Transformation". Reed
de me think of certain novels I
I do that in the chapter
so does such-and-such
ut to try and reduce it to three

was, in its very formulative
. Having already recorded
tes over the past three years
he other for Andy Warhol,
anned to write an album
gic: "I saw a man turn into a
er/I saw a man hang from
he jungles of the Amazon...
o me" ("Power And Glory"),
mine had told me about
y had seen, things they had
out on this album. And then

illnesses, and eventual
'Doc", the great R&B
who died last March;
only, "a friend, the last

with the original
his subject and I assign
ny business. I'm

me obvious to me
continue with it.

al confession.
er, spoken in
s have been
nose of friends
a kind of
n. "Magic And
d Rita, is the
ations at
"Sword
3 years
ncy
q
r
m

RIGHT: THE FRENCH MARKET HIM AS A ROBOT.

'What is there? Birth, life, death and the conflict in between. On *New York* I was trying to define a city, living in it, having children in it, survival. *Drella* introduced a person I really knew – I wanted to give you a feel for his life and what he was like. And this one? It's not where I'll hang my hat forever.' *Lou Reed*

'I love *Berlin*, and *Magic And Loss* is its closest descendant since. It's a coherent whole instead of 14 disparate songs. But *Berlin* was a noble attempt to deal with an old warhorse. Boy meets girl, loses girl, and there's no reunion. It was doomed right from the start. But I'm well past that person now. I've covered that, and it was in a different place. I haven't listened to my old records in a very long time, but I always

Manhattan transfer

From Warhol protégé to word processor — rock legend Lou Reed tells ROBERT SANDALL about his poetic approach to song lyrics

Thanks to an unholy alliance of indulgent publishers and gullible fans, it's not unusual any more to come across a rock star with literary pretensions. A rock star with serious literary credibility, though, is a rare creature indeed, and there are times when Lou Reed himself has problems acknowledging the impact his words have had. The idea, he explains, black leather jacket creaking, was always "to take a poet's or novelist's approach to the songs so that the lyrics could stand alone, but with the fun of the two guitars, bass and drums there to enhance them as well". The runaway success of this enterprise, however, seems to have come as a bit of a surprise.

He was, he says, "amazed and dumbstruck" to be presented last year with one of the 200 hand-printed editions of his lyrics ("from the Velvet Underground straight ...."), which circulated among ..... in pre-glasnost .... manager) ..... when ....ntation, ... hap-
..... ed,

ABOVE: LOU REED PUBLISHES HIS POETRY COLLECTION *BETWEEN THOUGHT AND EXPRESSION* AND RECEIVES HIS DUE AS A SERIOUS WRITER.

Reed: 'I was horrified that people were offended by my stuff and that I was causing some to be drug addicts.' M

....ect of his own influence, has ...d why some list.... ...rk ....

didn't want to be faced in the 1990s .... stuck in ...

typ....

tried to use some compassion. My characters, they may not be great people, but I give examples of their behaviour. I don't condemn them or take a moral stance. They're not terribly different from people everybody knows.' *Lou Reed*

'Writing involves an emotion that isn't in you. It's over there, in the work, and when you write – then you don't have it anymore. That's a loss too. Like maybe you gave up something you didn't want to surrender.' *Lou Reed*

'Lou Reed is the most underrated contemporary poet in America. He has [developed] a new form of expression. It's got natural rhythm to it, it's got pulse, it has a style about it . . . He has a kind of facility with language and a form of lyrical creativity that nobody else has. That's what makes it high art.' *Bob Ezrin, producer.*

A volume of Lou's lyrics and poems entitled Between Thought And Expression *was published in 1992.*

'I wanted to do my book for a very long time. It isn't a rock star's compilation. There's no pictures of my house or of the band. I didn't bring in some Belgian to paint the cover. It was serious. A lot of the lyrics only existed on record. I don't have drawers full of them, and I've thrown away the notebooks. I couldn't read the handwriting anyway. The songs are like my diary. If I want to know where I was, the book gives me a good idea.' *Lou Reed*

'Why don't Reed's words work *as words*? Chiefly because, unornamented they're too dumb, too simple, too obvious, too embarrassing . . . On record, "Heroin" is a momentous piece of work . . . The lyrics, which rely for their effect on the intonation Reed gives them as well as the musical juxtaposition, lose nearly everything in detachment. Oddly enough, the best pieces in *Between Thought And Expression* are the sarcastic incantations from *New York*, songs like "Common Ground", a warning against collusion with extremists, "Strawman" and "Busload Of Faith". Simple tricks of repetition, smart one-lines, grave anger, combine to produce polemic which has a definite life of its own.' *D.J. Taylor, The Modern Review*

'I wanted to approach songwriting with the input that a novelist might have, to create a strong visual image or a short story in a small number of words. Just because there are guitars and drums in there as well, doesn't mean it's stupid. It shouldn't be that every time you listen to a rock and roll record, the intelligent part of your mind switches off.' *Lou Reed*

'I'm thinking of trying to take the audience in a certain direction with me, and losing the audience that doesn't want to go that way. Because I don't want anyone coming in

Lou Reed, exuding sternness from behind steely spectacles. Hopes that benignity might have come with advancing years are soon dashed by his stage presence

Really cares a lot, but looks like he does not

THERE CANNOT be more than a ... n the world who ... le wearing a ... But

probably the best concept album, detailing reactions to the suffering and death of friends afflicted by terminal illness, released so far this year. But live entertainment it is not. Given the harrowing ... it would be unreasonable ... between

though I look like I do not," is a line ... stands out. It's about Warhol, but ...

| ROCK |
| BEN THOMPSON |

mythologising to touch down on British shores this week. The name **Beastie Boys** does not strike terror into VW owners like it used to, but that is probably no bad thing. Beastie-Boy image building was too effective for its own good; they ... convinced everyone of what ... they were, that when ...

Your Head, but for the moment ... the three of them, their ... benign DJ, H ... Yauch), ... park ...

LOU PLAYS THE WHOLE OF *MAGIC AND LOSS* LIVE ON A 1992 TOUR.

under false pretences.' *Lou Reed*

Following extensive worldwide promotional tours for the Magic And Loss *album during the first half of 1992, Lou followed up with some European 'greatest hits' shows – most notably a headlining slot at Britain's famous Glastonbury Festival. A musical anthology, also titled* Between Thought And Expression, *was subsequently released that summer – along with the* Magic And Loss *video. In the autumn, Lou joined in a celebratory concert at New York's Madison Square Garden to mark Bob Dylan's thirty years in the recording business. Reed was asked to perform his favourite Dylan composition.*

'I chose to play "Foot Of Pride", because I just got back from an eight-month tour. Once a day I would listen to it and just fall down laughing.' *Lou Reed*

Days later Lou joined Sterling Morrison on stage during a John Cale solo gig at Columbia University. This latter event led to inevitable rumours of a Velvet Underground reunion.

'I'm a lot less pigeon-holed than I was before. I try not to read [the press] stuff unless it's nice. So I don't read a whole lot. My wife censors it, says you don't need this impinging on your life.' *Lou Reed*

'I really believe that art is man at his highest. It really is an expression of the highest abilities, the greatest sensitivies. It is art you turn to, to heal, to make you feel better – and it's art you turn to for solutions.' *Lou Reed*

During 1992, it was the American politicians who were suddenly turning to art, or rather its creators, as Democrats and Republicans battled to increase their credibility amongst the TV watching, film-going and record-buying public. In the case of the latter, the Democrats seem to have traditionally held the balance of power with rock musicians – if not with their audiences.

Bob Dylan, of course, was once quoted in a Presidential inauguration speech – by the last Democratic President, Jimmy Carter. This time it was Lou's turn, not to be quoted in such grand fashion, but to be invited to play at the Tennessee Street Festival on 18 January 1993, a Presidential inaugural show to honour the home state of Albert Gore, Vice President-elect of the United States. Bearing in mind the often contentious nature of Lou's work, and the fact that Tipper Gore (Al's wife) had supported a campaign to clean up rock lyrics, Reed seems to have been an unlikely choice for such an event.

'I didn't think I was the first name that sprang to mind for an inaugural show!' *Lou Reed*

'The impression that I got about all that stuff about cleaning up rock lyrics, is that it's water under the bridge. Or else why would so many music business people have been supporting the Democrats? And on the other hand, she's welcome to her opinion. Whether she gets clout because of who her husband is, well, that's the American way, isn't it? Besides, if Bush had his way, there wouldn't be any records at all.' *Lou Reed*

'This is such a Puritan country. Someone asked John [Cougar] Mellencamp, who has a young daughter, "Would you let her hear this record that has a so-called obscenity?" He said, "Yes, and so what? It makes people aware of more things – that's called education." What is this terrible power?' *Lou Reed*

'I don't think people are that stupid. You can't ban things just because there are a couple of lunatics out there, committing suicide after they hear a Judas Priest record. You know, people aren't going to go into really hurtful sex acts because they go to a Mapplethorpe exhibition. It's just not the way it works.' *Lou Reed*

'I played at a Christmas party at Big Mike's, a sound rehearsal studio, and I did

Notes from the underground

D J Taylor

The Dostoevsky of rock: Lou Reed

For anyone born in the period 1958-62 who consequently began to listen to 'serious' pop in the early to

ed. In an England wh
album'—does anyone,
ber concept albums?—
artistic respectability an
of Pink Floyd's *The L*
Moon was commonly su
back some sort of creat
painful drone of a nur
Light/White Heat's title
the sacrilegious.

Ironically, the Velve
not even contemporary. I
lightning gear-changes
capable, it was nearly
Underground And Nico
day in early 1967; *Wh*
which contained the
of 'Sister Ray' ("How
for?" the recording e
to have enquired. "
band is supposed to h
towards the end of t
appeal to the listene
was almost wholly
much liked the s
putting out at th
dence of a

st rock per-
rmers wish to
e loved. Some
ill even dress
iewer, acting
d, easing the
able write-up.
vith personal-
ed wrote on
a, his recent
album with
"they're too
style."
time for the
iating circus
y that passes
ewing. Intro-
pt to a mum-
rush-off, and
cools to deep
s for the first
This is a man
l life has been
through the
songs. What
ay?
specifically
is re-visit his
f The Velvet
one of the
f rock history,
l's Factory in
y, full of its
ters, nascent
diarists. Any
on the sleazy
era will have
er source of
cause the sub-
nes to discuss
negotiation.
been many
the release of
ecord of 1973,
e most recent
rk and *Magic*
this refusal to
y would have
ossible for a
h so many
rs of his gen-
ed floundered
hat drowning
matter of time.
nly, the pieces
grouped into
made sense
d learned the
ts which en-
protect the
usic from the
cts of record-
maturity, the
looms in the
ng and angry
me useable as

Still resolved to walk on the wild side

David Toop talks to Lou Reed

about rock music for grown-ups

PETER TRIEVNOR

Lou Reed: poised for the first idiotic question

been working hard, Reed admits that the limitations of his chosen palette have irked him throughout his career.

"For some reason", he says, "folk, blues, jazz, certainly novels and the theatre, without even thinking about it, all have adult-oriented material.

nostalgia, perhaps You're certainly not gonna like the new versions of what you liked when you were 18 that are out now. There's no reason why you can't still like rock 'n' roll."

The adult-oriented material that Reed confronted on

was songwriter Doc Pomu
In his early years of comp
ing, Pomus wrote for Di
Big Joe Turner, The Drift
and Elvis Presley. As Re
points out, records such
"Save the Last Dance for M
"set a standard for a certa
kind of song. It established
certain kind of song on a le
that it might not have been
before. It's like a phra
that'll probably be wit
people for a very, very lor
time. It'll probably wend
way into the folk idiom."

This capacity to use
simple, popular form to
flect profound and fun
mental aspects of hum
experience has been a goal
Reed since his first song
The Velvet Undergro
Where his lyrics stan
literature can now be ju
from the publication
book, a collection of s
entitled *Between Th*
and Expression. Along
the sad and acerbic ta
drug addicts, transve
alcoholism and death
book also prints two
views. A fervent hater
interview process, Re
came the interrogat
order to speak to
Havel (a personal her
Hubert Selby, author
Exit to Brooklyn.

Havel showed Re
important these lyri
been to dissident Czec
vakians, who translate
and then handprinted
into small books which
distributed under thr
imprisonment. As Hav
to Reed during their m
in 1990, "music, u
ground music, in parti
one record by a band c
Velvet Underground, pl
a rather significant role ir
development of our coun

This realisation that
songs had contributed t
real freedom movement
overwhelms Reed, confir
ing his belief in the purpose
his work. "I really believe th
art is man at his hi
really is an expre
highest abilitie
sensitivities. I
to, to heal,

"Heroin". I prefaced it by saying, 'We're going to do a song called "Heroin", but I don't want anybody who overdoses in the bathroom, to blame it on this song.' *Lou Reed*

'I don't keep up with politics enough, to really speak that knowledgeably about it.' *Lou Reed*

'If we can go into Somalia, why can't we go into New York? Maybe we should be putting all that effort into the cities of America. I still live here, and I'm not leaving. I love New York. I can't stand to see the fact that it keeps going on getting worse . . . Instead of closing all those army bases, why not keep the army at its present level and use them: build roads, clean up cities, patrol things. They don't have to be there for just wartime things.' *Lou Reed*

'I have no idea [about Bill Clinton]. I don't know him. I didn't see him play saxophone, but if he could play like Boots Randolph [the Nashville studio musician who had a hit with "Yakety Sax"], that would be fine. I think your hopes can go up a little bit if someone plays a musical instrument, although I'm sure we'll find out that Hitler played something. Oh, that's right, he painted.' *Lou Reed*

'People say Lou Reed is too serious. So shoot me, I'm playing for keeps.' *Lou Reed*

With Bill Clinton safely in the White House, Lou disappeared back to the rehearsal rooms, playing privately with John Cale, Sterling Morrison and Mo Tucker. After a professional life-time of highs and lows, it looked like a remarkable climax was about to be reached. Cale always said that Lou and he never really capitalised on the ability held within the ranks of the

Tough Shit

On his new record, Lou Reed turns an unblinking eye to the devastation wrought by death. But now there's a keynote in his work that many might not expect from the legendary founder of The Velvet Underground. "It's compassion," he tells Mark Cooper. "I really *like* people."

Velvet Underground. So would there yet be a reunion? When Cale was interviewed on US television early in 1993, the suggestion was that it would happen. With remarkable rapidity during the Spring of 1993, rumours of a private reunion coalesced first into a confirmation that the reconstituted Velvet Underground would play in Paris in June. This was quickly followed by confirmation of dates in Britain, Holland, Germany and the United States. There were reports of a possible new album, as well as promises of a whole series of re-packaged and previously unre-leased Velvet Underground material. At the time of writing, in April 1993, it appears that Lou Reed's involvement with the Velvet Underground is anything but the spent force it seemed to be more than twenty years ago. The only question now is . . . how long can it last?

'What are the constants of Lou Reed music? That I did the best I could with what I've got. And, oh yeah, I meant every word of it.' Lou Reed

Acknowledgements

Special thanks are due to Glen Marks for his expertise and help in the preparation of this book and for making the Glen Marks Archive available for source material and illustrations. Thanks are also due to Bill Allerton for archive material, and to the following for supplying photographs: Claude Gassian (pp. 9, 70-71, 88, 90, 115, 125, 143), Mick Rock (pp. 53, 55, 57, 73, 86, 89), Gerard Malanga, Robert Ellis, Words, Retna Pictures, MGM Verve, RCA Records, Arista Records, Honda Scooters. Thanks are also due the following publications: *Best, Creem, Disc, 18, The Evening Standard, Event, The Face, Friendz, Fusion, High Times, The Independent, The Independent on Sunday, International Musician, International Times, Interview, Let It Rock, Melody Maker, The Modern Review, NY Rocker, New Musical Express, New York Post, Penthouse, Punk, Q, Rock and Folk, Rocket, Rolling Stone, Sounds, Stimula Books, The Sunday Times, Time Out, Village Voice, Zigzag.* The publishers would also like to thank Philip Lloyd Smee for his enthusiasm, support and imaginative design